A Comparative Investigation
of Economic Systems
& Corresponding Environmental
Effects

A Comparative Investigation of Economic Systems & Corresponding Environmental Effects

Mark J. Davern

A COMPARATIVE INVESTIGATION OF ECONOMIC SYSTEMS & CORRESPONDING ENVIRONMENTAL EFFECTS

iUniverse books may be ordered through booksellers or by contacting:

iUniverse
1663 Liberty Drive
Bloomington, IN 47403
www.iuniverse.com
844-349-9409

ISBN: 978-0-5953-9526-2 (sc)
ISBN: 978-0-5958-3925-4 (e)

Print information available on the last page.

iUniverse rev. date: 11/16/2020

Dedicated to

the Advancement of our Kind

and

the Respect of other Kinds

Contents

Preface

This is dedicated to all the cultures that are being supplanted by the current free-trade global economic system.

Every culture has certain undeniably valuable characteristics that have evolved socially and biologically in particular geographic and climatic regions of the earth. It would be a shame to not notice that they were being increasingly marginalized by the current global economic system. If we are to maintain viability and stability in our species, there has to be re-orientation towards these cultures. After all, diversity is the basis of stability in biology and it should be with respect to culture too.

Hopefully in this book, I will be able to suggest new ways our species can relate so that these cultures can persist onwards and at the same time contribute meaningfully to the species as a whole. At once, it seems as though there might be significant improvements with regards to eliminating potential conflicts between current dominant cultures and current subordinate cultures. Under a more appropriate economic system, everyone would be afforded the opportunity to live **their** way of life without unnecessary subordination of each other's cultures.

Acknowledgments

Thanks to everyone who helped me organize and formulate the best manner in which the study was to be done. Especially, Dr. Magdol who understood the concepts and helped me to better categorize the variables and procedure of the report.

Special thanks to Dr. Shryock who showed an interest in my project and agreed to sign on as my major professor. Although heavily criticized during my presentation, Dr. Shryock was supportive and made suggestions on the manner in which the project could be pursued.

Thanks to the Social Sciences Interdisciplinary Department. Ms. Pearles, Jakowlaszak, & DiSalvo and Dr. Dryden, who was always interested in hearing from me, were very helpful whenever I needed information and/or advice. Fortunately, I have completed a master's degree in Social Sciences with a true mixture of anthropological, philosophical, geographical, and sociological disciplines.

Thanks again,
M. J. Davern

Abstract

The following paper is a cross-cultural analysis of various selected cultures. It analyzes and categorizes different modes of procurement or production and their economic systems. Modes of procurement are categorized as interdependent economic systems. Modes of production are categorized as independent economic systems. (Note: Some of the cultures analyzed have both interdependent procuring economic activity and independent producing economic activity.)

Modes of procurement, which produce interdependent economic systems, will correspond with distinct environmental conditions, as will independent economies with their modes of production. The environmental conditions analyzed are social, physical, and biological aspects of the environment. Social environmental variables include population size, level of social emotion, sociopolitical structure, and magnitude of sharing (public ownership) or private ownership.

The physical environmental variables will measure: 1) existence or non-existence of pollution, and 2) degree of alteration and/or manipulation of environment.

The biological environment will vary on: 1) the level of biodiversity, measured in the relative abundance (endangerment and/or extinction) of other species, and 2) the abundance in numbers, and 3) presence or absence of domesticated species.

The study concludes with an analysis of the cultures, and findings of the social, physical, and biological environments of each of the cultures. Independent economies are proposed to have social environments that are: 1) high in population, 2) low in social emotion, 3) hierarchical political structure, inherited or established, and 4) private ownership.

The physical environment of independent economies is predicted to be: 1) polluted due to wasteful practices, and 2) altered and/or manipulated, more so than societies that operate under interdependent economies.

The biological environment of independent economies is expected to be: 1) low in biodiversity (through either high human population or exploitation, endangerment and extinction of other species), 2) low in abundance within individual species, and 3) high in domestication of other species (which is a kind of exploitation).

Conversely, the social environment of interdependent economies is expected to be: 1) low or moderate in population, 2) high in social emotion, 3) hierarchical political structure, egalitarian or achieved and temporary, and 4) high in sharing and public ownership.

The physical environment will be characterized by: 1) little or no polluting practices, and 2) little or no alteration of physical environment.

The biology of interdependent economies is predicted to be: 1) high in biodiversity (through low human population and/or little exploitation and endangerment of other species), 2) high in abundance, and 3) low in domestication of other species.

Introduction

Humans have existed for many millennia. From the earliest known human ancestors, Australopithecus and Zinjanthropus boisei, which mean Southern Ape and East African Man respectively, to the first Homo ancestors, Homo habilus, Homo erectus, and archaic Homo sapiens, humans have lived in relative harmony with other species of the planet in an interdependent web of life. Until recently, about 10-15 thousand years ago, human subsistence systems have been in accordance with what the local, distant (viá trade), and regional ecosystems could provide for them and other species in the environment.

With the advent of agriculture, humans were able to alter the natural restraints of the environment. One of these restraints was the female hunter-gatherer's 4-year birth-interval between offspring. With a dependence on food production vs. food gathering, agricultural females could have 2, 3, or 4 children *within* the normal food gathering female's 1 child in 4 years birth-interval. Anyone can see that this shift in subsistence technology brought on the beginnings of the population explosion.[1]

As Homo sapiens begin to rely on themselves in providing themselves with the means of subsistence, they begin to show something completely extraordinary with respect to other species on earth. They begin to live in a sense *more independently* of nature, thus breaking through & beyond the interdependence of earth's ecosystem. Humankind begins to live *apart from* nature, no longer *a part of* nature. Consequently, the social environment of humanity, and the biological and physical environment of earth (the ecology) are impaired.

---

1. Leakey, Richard E. and Roger Lewin, <u>People of the Lake: Mankind & Its Beginnings</u>, p. 137.

1

- (Note: What I mean by living more independently of nature is that
throughout history some of humanity has increasingly been able to gain a
certain degree of autonomy (or independence) from the natural world by
altering (or alleviating) the constraints of nature and by increasing their
ability to produce their own subsistence.)

Statement of Purpose

In the midst of increasing threats to the environment, exponential population growth, resource depletion, and pollution, our relationship to the world is in need of reflection. How has humanity *suddenly* increased numbers to unprecedented levels? To find an answer, we must analyze various economic systems, corresponding ideologies, and subsequent behaviors, in relation to nature. Our present circumstances are consequences of our past ideologies and behavior, which form the basis of our existing economic systems.

Hominid evolution began when we left the rainforest regions of Africa, moved into the tropical woodlands, and eventually into the open savanna. This movement, whether by choice or in reaction to external pressure, created a new ecological niche for the evolution of our species.[2]

Our behavior, at first, was probably similar to the behavior of our closest forerunners—apes, chimpanzees, and other primates. The specific kinds of behavior I am interested in, for this research, are modes of procurement *and* modes of production. In other words, how do humans behave towards the environment (and how are they disposed, ideologically) when they obtain the means (resources) of survival? Do they *procure* by hunting, gathering, fishing or scavenging for subsistence, thereby living *interdependently* with nature? Or do they *produce* the means of subsistence by breeding animals, planting crops, or manufacturing objects, thereby living *more* independently of nature or *more* self-reliant?

The first set of behaviors represents *modes of procuring* from the environment. These behaviors could be considered interdependent in nature. They are interdependent because humankind obtains resources from the environ-

---

2. Campbell, Bernard, <u>Human Ecology</u>, p. 25.

ment by a lesser degree of manipulation and/or alteration, but, more so to the extent that the environment allows or provides naturally.[3] By a lesser degree of manipulation, I mean that the extent to which humans actively produce their subsistence through manipulation of the land, water, air, and/or other natural resources is relatively minimal, when compared to more complex economies such as agriculture, full pastoralism, and industry.

The second set of behaviors represents *modes of production.* This set of human behaviors is characterized by a diminished need to depend *directly* on *nature* to provide subsistence and an increased dependence on *humanity* to obtain subsistence. Humans begin to rely more on their *own ingenuity* in manipulating the environment to *produce* a *surplus* of resources *beyond* what the environment would *otherwise* provide naturally.

As humans increasingly gain independence in obtaining their subsistence, they *perceive* nature as subordinate and begin to *act* rather insensitively towards it. This has led to an increased exploitation and pollution of the environment. These kinds of acts can damage earth's life systems, and could, ultimately destroy humanity itself.

One of the primary purposes of this book is to reveal how independent subsistence systems have led to negative effects on various aspects of the environment, *and* humanity itself.

---

3.   Campbell, p. 134.

Methods

The research technique I used for this paper was a cross-cultural comparative method. At first, I wanted to do a random sample so that a statistical analysis could be done. However, I was unable to gain access to a proper sample universe categorized by subsistence economy. Therefore, I took a purposively selected sample of various cultures with different subsistence techniques, ranging from very interdependent to very independent in nature.

The problem with doing a purposive sample is that a probability test cannot legitimately be done. At a future time perhaps a statistical analysis can be done, if a true random sample is taken.

The problem that often arose, when I tried to categorize for myself a universe of cultures from various sources, like the *The Illustrated Encyclopedia of Mankind*[4] or *Encyclopedia of World Cultures*,[5] was that some cultures practiced more than one subsistence pattern. It was especially difficult to categorize a culture when it practiced *both* an interdependent technique, i.e. hunting, and an independent technique, i.e. agriculture. As shown later, some of the cultures selected *do* practice both hunting and gathering along with agriculture.

This problem of mixed economies was similar to another study that I did last year. That time, I wanted to compare the subsistence economies of nations, not cultures. Soon after beginning, I ran into the problem of several cultures within one nation, each practicing various subsistence techniques. Therefore, it was impossible to categorize any one nation as having an interdependent subsistence technique or an independent technique. This time, I can-

---

4. *Illustrated Encyclopedia of Mankind, The,* Richard Carlisle Ed., Thematic Index, Vol. 22, pp. 2862-2877.
5. *Encyclopedia of World Cultures*, David Levinson Ed., Subject Index, Vol. 10, pp. 79-322.

not even classify one culture as having a *wholly* interdependent or independent economic system.

However, I can establish a *gradient* of subsistence technique, in other words, culture A is very interdependent, relatively interdependent or has a true mix of interdependent procurement *and* independent production. Culture B, as compared with A, is relatively independent in economic provisioning, but relatively interdependent, when compared with C (an industrial society).

Concepts, Definitions, and Indicators

The term economic system is defined as the ways in which humankind has arranged for its material provisioning.[6] Economic systems range in complexity from hunting and gathering to modern industrial economies. The underlying essence of any economic system is the coordination, on the part of the individuals of the society, of activities, a set of behaviors associated with material provisioning. This coordination of activities could be termed a mode of procurement *or* a mode of production.

The emphasis on *(or)* is intentional. While researching for this paper, I encountered the term *mode of procurement,* used to signify *all* human subsistence patterns or techniques. This terminology appeared to be similar to the common term, mode of production, but in addition, had the undertone of procurement, all in one. This observation gave me the insight to conceptualize subsistence economies in a whole new way.

Usually, the term "mode of production" is utilized to signify various subsistence economies. During my research, many of the authors utilized another term: "modes of procurement." Instead of utilizing just mode of procurement *or* just mode of production to indicate subsistence economies, I thought it would be more accurate to distinguish certain economies as using modes of procurement and other economies as using modes of production. For this study, hunting, fishing, gathering, and transhumance, are defined as modes of procurement. Full pastoralism, agriculture, and industrialism are defined as modes of production.

---

6.   Halperin, Rhoda H., <u>Cultural Economies: Past and Present</u>, p. 8.

Modes of procurement are different from modes of production in that the manner in which humans obtain material provisions from the environment is *interdependent* with nature. The term interdependent means that humans extract the resources from earth in a manner that is: 1) not significantly and/or harmfully altering to the earth, and 2) not beyond the boundaries of what the environment provides naturally.[7]

On the other hand, *production modes* are the foundations of independent economic systems. Characteristically, these modes of behavior: 1) significantly alter and/or harm the local and (sometimes) global environment, and 2) are *exploitive* in nature, by extracting resources *beyond* what the environment would otherwise provide *naturally*.

The difference between interdependent systems and independent systems is in the manner in which humans *actively produce a surplus* in an independent economy, or *passively procure a subsistence* in an interdependent economy. Independent systems will tend to *significantly alter* the environment *and potentially harm* it, while interdependent systems will tend to *not significantly alter the environment* and *maintain biodiversity and stability* in the ecosystem.

The terms independent and interdependent are used to categorize types of economic systems and their typical behavioral modes, which are either procurement or production. These behavioral modes are supported by a culture's ideological perceptions, values and/or dispositions towards others and the environment.[8,9] According to Altman, humankind has three dispositions (world-views) towards the environment: 1) afraid of and below the environment, 2) apart from and above the environment, or 3) equal to and a part of the environment.[10]

Independent economic systems, e.g. full pastoralism, agriculture, and industrialism, correspond with Altman's *apart from and above* world-view of the environment.[11] As consequence of this world-view/disposition, behaviors that are increasingly independent of nature arise. What I mean by independent is that humans: 1) increasingly perceive nature and other species as *below themselves*, and therefore, to be controlled in a manner which serves their

7.   Altman, Irwin, <u>Culture and Environment</u>, p. 15.
8.   Ryle, Gilbert, "*From* <u>The Concept of Mind</u>." In <u>What is an Emotion?</u>, Cheshire Calhoun and Robert C. Solomon eds., pp. 256-257, 262.
9.   Steward, Julian, <u>Theory of Culture Change</u>, p. 37.
10. Altman, Irwin, p. 15.
11. Altman, p. 15.

interests *over* the interests of others, and 2) increasingly are able to provide their own subsistence, affording them a certain degree of autonomy from nature, thereby distanciating themselves emotionally from nature. Below I will illustrate what I mean by an emotional distanciation of humankind from nature by using principles of biology.

Richard E. Leakey postulated in his 1994 book, The Origin of Humankind, that three revolutions mark the history of life on earth.[12]

First was the origin of life itself. "Life, in the form of microorganisms, became a powerful force in a world where previously only chemistry and physics had operated."[13] The next was the origin of multicellular organisms, about a half billion years ago. Plants and animals of different forms and sizes interacted in fertile ecosystems. And lastly, life becomes aware of itself, with the origin of human-consciousness, about 2.5 million years ago.[14]

The first revolution, the origin of life itself, and the second, the origin of multicellular organisms, were critical in developing the theory that humankind's biological bond with the rest of nature, and even with other members of its own species, has been severed. Leakey states that *before* life, there was just chemistry and physics, operating.[15]

Then it dawned on me, that, in fact, is it not *chemistry and physics* that life itself is operating under? Also, just as there were physical and chemical bonds that held the molecules of microorganisms together should there not be chemical and physical bonds between multicellular organisms, i.e. other life forms, consisting of chemistry and physics, interacting in one interdependent web of life. Why would this interaction and unification of chemistry and physics between matter disintegrate with the dawning of multicellular life, which can be considered as just a more complex form of chemistry and physics?

The chemical component of these bonds is represented by emotions. Emotions, as triggered by perception, are in fact chemical releases/responses to the thing perceived.[16] Therefore, when we disconnect ourselves chemically from other life forms (other species) by adopting a more independent disposition

---

12. Leakey, Richard E., The Origin of Humankind, p. 139.
13. Leakey, p. 139.
14. Ibid.
15. Leakey, The Origin of Humankind, p. 139.
16. Damasio, Antonio, Descartes' Error: Emotion, Reason, and the Human Brain, pp. 131-132.

towards these species, we distanciate ourselves emotionally from the rest of nature, and the sympathetic bonds that originally existed between the two.

This emotional distanciation is a relatively recent phenomenon. For millions of years, *before* humanity gained the ability to significantly free itself from living *within* the constraints of the natural world, humans had no choice, or had yet to realize a choice, and had to accept living within the constraints of nature, which subsequently meant that they must remain fundamentally and sympathetically connected to various species on which they relied upon directly and immediately for survival.

It is not as if we, today, do not fundamentally and *ultimately* rely upon other species for survival, but that the *directness and immediateness* of that reliance has been *assuaged* by a market system, and is no longer apparent. This obscurity, in turn, *desensitizes* the bonds between humans and other species. Consequently, the emotionally-sympathetic connections that once existed under a *more direct and urgent* economy have also been obscured. Consequently, the creatures that we ultimately rely on *for survival* are treated rather *insensitively* (e.g. meat production plants, fur-trading, etc.). This consequently, has led to many of the over-exploitation, over-population, and pollution problems we experience today.

Interdependent cultures, by virtue of their continued chemically, physically, biologically, and *visibly* needed connection between themselves and other species in their environment and to the extent that their community practices reciprocity between themselves and other members of their community, effectively *maintain* and *strengthen* the biological bonds (bio-bonds) between life forms, and between each other.[17] These bonds are maintained and strengthened because the people have an immediate *biological need* of the prey species *and* others in the community by virtue of the integral part they play in an interdependent economy.[18] Although modern economies are based on the production of domesticated species for consumption, which thereby creates a need for them, the potency of the need is usually mitigated by a readily available surplus supply, which is usually unavailable in primitive economies. Therefore, it could be fair to suppose that people who live in procuring economies will *appreciate* prey species more than people who live in mass producing

---

17. Leakey & Lewin, <u>People of the Lake: Mankind & Its Beginnings</u>, pp. 92, 113, & 137.
18. Reader, p. 146.

and storing economies. A readily available surplus supply serves to *obfuscate* the *real need* of prey (domesticated) species to humans in a market economy.

In an economy based on hunting and gathering, the hunted species, the gathered species, and (if sharing is the norm) the fellow community members, *all* have a *direct, immediate, and integral* part to play in ensuring the survival of an individual. Whereas, in increasingly independent economies, such as a market economy, the contributions of individuals are *pooled and indirectly* received from a redistributive central government.[19] In an interdependent economy contributions from individuals, as stated above, are *directly* received in an immediate and personal manner. It is therefore, *(more apparently)* essential for an individual to maintain the biological bonds between the members of his/her species and the members of other species in an interdependent economic system. It is only when humans, *seemingly,* no longer need others *(immediately, directly, and personally)* for survival, (either of their own species or of other species), that the physical, chemical, and biological bonds between the two are weakened.

Compliance, Religion & Social Emotion

All modes of production and/or procurement rely on social rewards and/or penalties to keep the actors of the economic system in compliance. Traditional societies base compliance on "communal expressions of approval or disapproval."[20] Communal expressions are founded on social emotions.[21] Social emotions are essential to the proper functioning of social groups that modern economic systems have *increasingly* supplanted with external controls.

Modern economic systems, instead, rely on objective forms of currency (or money) and institutions of punishment to gain compliance. In traditional economies, people are regulated by social emotions. Guilt, shame, pride, and empathy all play a role in getting a miscreant to *feel* bad, and subsequently, reform and comply.[22]

---

19. Polanyi, p. 149.
20. Bornstein, Morris, Comparative Economic Systems: Models and Cases, pp. 25 & 27.
21. Ekman, Paul, "Biological and Cultural Contributions to the Body and Facial Movement in the Expression of Emotions," in Explaining Emotions. Amelie Oksenberg Rorty ed., pp. 73-99.
22. Leakey & Lewin, p. 137.

Therefore, in modern systems official monitoring of behavior becomes a major concern because internally, socially-regulating emotions are not there, consequently many times the actor does not *feel* bad. Often, the wrong-doer is *not* moved emotionally to change his/her behavior and I argue that true behavior modification requires an emotional base. Instead he/she is moved *physically* by brute force under a modern economy. This sometimes happens only after severe casualties and/or injuries have resulted and requires continual regulation and maintenance. This is primarily because the wrong-doer does not feel bad about his/her actions. The reason the wrong-doer does not *feel* bad is because the emotional bonds have been severed, between *people, other species,* and *the environment,* at large.

In traditional systems, these emotional bonds remain not only in tact, but are strengthened each time one member of the group *relies on* another member of the group for **biological** survival, in an economic system of reciprocity.[23] At its inception, these bonds are firmly rooted in humankind's relationship to the environment *and* each other. *These* bonds serve to prevent the population from wrong-doing and free them from continuous monitoring, as institutions and/ or material/monetary incentives do in modern societies.[24]

To the extent that these *systems of compliance* represent the morality of a society, I would like them to be a measure of the society's religious character. In modern systems, just as institutions of punishment are present to monitor misbehavior, institutions of religion are present to monitor immoral behavior. Whereas interdependent societies regulate behavior more through internal social control in emotion, modern, independent societies use more external measures to maintain morality in society with a clergy, ecclesiastic institutions, and well-defined rules, etc. Hence, we begin to see the proliferation of churches and formal written religious laws (e.g. the Bible) in increasingly independent economies. Whereas, in interdependent societies, informal, unwritten laws (i.e. taboos & totems) prevail.[25]

Although, perhaps traditional societies have very few written moral rules due to a lack of literacy. On the other hand, these societies could conceivably *evolve* such abilities, if there arose *the need* for them. In fact, perhaps it was *this*

---

23. Reader, p. 146.
24. Bornstein, p. 23.
25. Leakey & Lewin, p. 190.

very need to *explicitly*, inscribe moral rules for society that *caused literacy to arise* in the first place, in increasingly independent economies.[26]

In interdependent societies, where moral rules are enforced *more implicitly* than explicitly, in obligatory kinship networks,[27] everyday, routine interaction,[28] and the like, where the economy is based *more on generalized reciprocity* than on centralized redistribution, the need *does not arise* yet to express morality in formal, written rules. Because social emotion and communal expressions of approval or disapproval are sufficient enough to keep the population moral, there may *not* be a need yet for *external institutions* of morality to arise. Morality is included within the immediate, direct and personal economic activities of daily life, which concomitantly means that morality is automatically incorporated *within* their economic system.[29,30]

Heilbroner appropriately recognizes the secondary priority that a capitalist mass production economy, i.e. an independent economy, places on moral behavior. First priority is profit, while second priority is *how you attain it*. Also, since the system relies mainly on external monitoring, there are *bound to be* quite a few cheaters that go undetected.[31] And, in so far as the cheater is not detected and a profit is obtained, it is considered an acceptable loss. One could say that the system is relatively tolerant of immoral behavior, and that moral behavior is secondary to the bottom line, monetary gain. This obviously gives precedence to materials over morality.

So, the relative presence or absence of functioning social emotions should indicate or coincide with the degree to which formality in religion is established. Formality can be measured by the existence of outside places of worship, i.e. temples, churches, etc., and/or explicitly written moral rules. Cultures that utilize mainly social emotions to gain compliance will have less of a need for formal institutions or rules of religion, thereby have few explicitly religious institutions or concepts. An informal religion prevails in these cul-

---

26. As with the Egyptian, Sumerian, & Mayan civilizations.
27. Basch, etal., Nations Unbound, p. 165.
28. Hannerz, Ulf, Cultural Complexity: Studies in the Social Organization of Meaning, Hannerz' form of life, p. 47.
29. Leakey & Lewin, pp. 176-177.
30. Polanyi, p. 148.
31. Boyd, Robert and Peter J. Richerson, "Punishment Allows the Evolution of Cooperation (or Anything Else) in Sizable Groups", in *Ethology and Sociobiology*, Vol. 13, pp. 171-195.

tures, where moral behavior is checked on a daily basis, *rather implicitly*, by social emotions of guilt, shame, sympathy, and moral-indignation.[32] Increasingly independent economies will correlate with low-levels of social emotion, and consequently, more often have *externally manifested* and *explicitly stated* religious institutions and concepts.

The presence of functioning social emotion within a society can be indicated by threats of ostracism from the group,[33] fear of offending others by threats to integrity,[34] and even, fear of offending other animals.[35] In contrast, a relative weakness of socio-emotional bonds in a culture can be indicated by: 1) rare instances of threatening to ostracize individuals from the group, and 2) heedlessness in causing harm to nature and/or dominating other species of nature, which can be named over-exploitation and domestication, respectively.

The case of offending other animals is particularly relevant for our study. The socio-emotional bonds that unite the people of traditional society seem to be extended to unite them *even* with other species of the environment and the environment itself. In this way, the social bonds are not exclusive to humans but extend outwards towards other species making them *inter-special* bonds.

It is not only the relative weakness of social bonds between members of the community, but also of the social bonds between humans and other species, and, between humans and the environment at large that allows modern economic systems to devastate local, regional, and sometimes global ecological systems. The social and even biological (to the extent that man depends[36] on prey species' for survival[37]) bonds between other species, the environment, and humanity, in traditional economic systems, seem to foster *profound* sympathetic emotions. I believe the strength of these emotions can grow so strong that they become biological, and then, spiritual. These spiritual bonds can be defined as a kind of connection that goes beyond *mere* survival of *body* to the

---

32. Leakey & Lewin, p. 137.
33. Leakey & Lewin, pp. 44, 133.
34. Gudykunst, William B., <u>Bridging Differences</u>, pp. 142-144.
35. Reader, p. 138.
36. Dependence creates the bonding between man and prey.
37. The bond, having consequences on survival, may develop a biological component within it.

survival of *soul*. This phenomenon may be what so many traditional societies describe as the spiritual bonds between themselves and environment.[38]

To demonstrate the *different magnitudes* of effect of each type of economy on environment, the following passage should be helpful:

> If hunters in a hunting and gathering economy were introduced to fire arms and other modern tools and methods of exploitation, the effects on environment will increase in kind to the sophistication level of the tools and methods introduced. This is the most important difference between *misbehaving* primitive hunters and a *misbehaving* well-tooled modern hunter. The impact of a misbehaving well-equipped technologically advanced hunter can be *far greater* than the impact of a misbehaving but relatively ill-equipped traditional hunter-gatherer. Even if a primitive hunter is *basely* immoral, the over-all negative effect on the environment will be negligible due to his/her primitive tools and methods.

The previous passage points out that it is important to note that *economies of scale* can damage ecological systems *far more so* than mere *subsistence economies*.

It is the primary focus of this book to analyze the social, physical, and biological differences of environment between societies that operate under interdependent economies versus independent economies. We should expect to see independent economies correlating with social, physical, and biological environments that are characterized as mainly destructive, in general, and in specific: 1) high in population, 2) low in social emotion, 3) represented by a hierarchical political structure, inherited or established 4) high levels of private ownership, 5) polluted, 6) altered and/or manipulated, more so than societies operating under interdependent economies, 7) low in biodiversity and abundance within species, and 8) high in the occurrence of domesticated species.

Interdependent economies are expected to strengthen and foster the overall health and viability of each of the environments to be investigated. These economies should be characterized by: 1) low levels of human population, 2) high levels of social emotion, 3) an egalitarian or achieved and temporary, hierarchical political structure, 4) high levels of sharing and public property, 5) relatively low levels of pollution, 6) low levels of manipulation/alteration of the environment, 7) high biodiversity, 8) high levels of abundance within species,

---

38. McGaa, Ed "Eagle Man", <u>Native Wisdom: Perceptions of the Natural Way</u>, p. 29.

and 9) a minimal occurrence of domesticated species. Whether interdependent or independent, the social, biological, and physical environments should correlate in distinctive ways with the type of economy.

Independent Variables: Subsistence Economy & Supportive Ideology

The independent variables are the ideology and the subsistence economy (or economic system) of a given culture. In the book, two ideological world-views: 1) equal to and a part of nature and 2) apart from and above nature, and five economic systems have been investigated, which are increasingly independent as follows: 1) hunting and gathering, 2) transhumance, 3) agriculture (limited, extensive, and intensive), 4) full pastoralism, and 5) industrialism.

The first two cultures, representing *mainly interdependent systems*, will be the Micmac hunting, fishing, and gathering people of the maritime provinces of eastern Canada in the 16th, 17th, and 18th centuries, and the Saami reindeer herders of northern Europe, originally hunters, who adopted transhumance three-to-four hundred years ago.[39] Both of these cultures maintain primarily "equal to and a part of nature" world-views.

Hunting-fishing and/or gathering economies are typically the most interdependent economies in which humans hunt, fish, and gather for their subsistence. It is interdependent because the people *generally* are not looking for a surplus production of resources; therefore, harm to other species and environment is minimal. The primary goal is to hunt, fish, and gather primarily what is *necessary* for survival. Therefore, it can truly be labeled *a subsistence economy*. Cases where surpluses are hunted/fished, gathered, and stored may have a greater impact on the environment, however, the human population is usually

---

39. Paine, Robert, <u>Herds of the Tundra: A Portrait of Saami Reindeer Pastoralism</u>, p. 13.

low *or* within the support boundaries of the local environment, and/or the technology and methodology used is not sufficient enough to do extensive damage.

Transhumance is the second most interdependent economy and it also is an example of an "equal to and a part of nature" economy. It is an economy located between hunter-gatherer economies and full pastoral economies. It is described as a non-interfering nomadic following of animal herds.[40] In this way, it is very much like a hunting and gathering economy.[41]

Under transhumance, humans do not domesticate, control the animals' migrations, or control breeding. However, they do protect the herd from predators, which creates an interdependence between the two. The herder simply follows the herd,[42] on a symbiotic journey. Whether the animals migrate continuously, or at different seasons, the transhumant will follow them, using a strategy based on mutual interdependence.

The second set of cultures will represent increasingly independent economies and ideologies. Once again, the Saami will be analyzed, but this time after incorporation into a market economy, which turns transhumance, a predominantly interdependent economy, into (what I call) production pastoralism. It can also be referred to as intensive pastoralism, full (domesticated) pastoralism, and/or husbandry.[43,44]

The ideology of the Saami changes *fundamentally* under the new economic system from "equal to and a part of nature" to "apart from and above nature". Their behavior also changes as they begin to purposely breed populations of reindeer for slaughter as opposed to following them and procuring them for subsistence. Once again, this type of pastoralism is interested in *producing a surplus*, whereas, transhumance is primarily interested in *procuring a subsistence* for survival. *This is the fundamental difference between the two pastoral economies.*

Production pastoralism is an economy that is based on breeding, protecting, and controlling a domesticated species. The herder remains in close contact with the herd species, whereas, under transhumance, the herd is allowed to roam, *more independently*, while the herder follows.[45] The herder does not, however, lose track of the animal.

---

40. Campbell, p. 135.
41. Beach, Hugh, <u>Reindeer-Herd Management in Transition</u>, p. 35.
42. Campbell, p. 136.
43. Beach, p. 36.
44. Campbell, p. 137.
45. Beach, p. 35.

There is a good reason why pastoralism is analyzed twice. The difference between transhumance and full pastoralism, as mentioned above, is fundamental to our study. Transhumance is a *mode of procurement* while full pastoralism is a *mode of production*, which will correspond with *a different set of social, physical, and biological environments* than transhumance. One such difference is on the biological environment.

Under full pastoralism, the breeding and increased size of the herd leaves less pasture area for other herbivores, which could reduce fauna in the region.[46] Also, a more intensive protection of the herd reduces a vital prey resource for predators.[47] This could disturb the health and balance of the ecosystem.[48]

The next cultures analyzed will be characterized by even *more independence.* The Mohave of the Colorado River basin, circa 1850, represent a rather mixed economic system of interdependence *and* independence. Practicing *limited agriculture* on the naturally fertile banks of the Colorado, while continuing to hunt, fish, and gather, the Mohave represent a minimally independent economy. Their ideology is also characterized by *a more "apart from and above nature" perception.*

The Nubians of Southern Egypt, who have been practicing extensive agriculture for millennia, on the other hand, represent *a truly agricultural society.* Their ideology and behavior represent a good contrast to the Mohave, who are *rather interdependent* when compared to Nubians.

The Taiwanese will represent an intensive agricultural economy, which rapidly turned industrial by the second half of the twentieth century. This was only done so effectively by the independent ideology of the central government that just pervaded the entire island. Again, the agriculture and eventual industrial economy of the Taiwanese will represent *another worthy contrast* to both the Nubian's and the Mohave' agricultural economies. This final culture will represent *the most independent economic system* of our study.

---

46. Campbell, p. 138.
47. Beach, p. 50.
48. Ibid., p. 229.

Dependent Variables: Social and Ecological Environments of Interdependent and Independent Economies

Social Environments of Interdependent vs. Independent Systems

The social environment of an interdependent system will contain the following: 1) an informal religion, indicating that morality and social emotions are inclusive of the economic system, 2) an egalitarian social structure, 3) interdependence with others as represented by generalized sharing of resources, and 4) low to moderate population size.

On the other hand, independent economic systems will have: 1) a formal religion, indicating that morality and social emotions are separate from the economic system, 2) a hierarchical social structure, 3) independence from others as represented by an increase in private ownership and a decrease of generalized resource sharing, and 4) a high population size for the region.

Physical Environment: Interdependent vs. Independent Systems

The physical environment of an interdependent economic system is usually not altered drastically. It should be characterized by: 1) a minimal altering of landscape (i.e. forests turned into prairies, and swamps filled to make solid soil, mountains cutout for mining, etc.), and 2) relatively no pollution. Nature reserves and/or parks will be rare, because people don't need them! The lack of manipulation and pollution maintains a healthy environment.

On the other hand, independent economic systems are expected to alter the physical environment significantly. These systems will affect the physical environment by: 1) altering or manipulating it, and 2) polluting it. These systems will also have parks and reserves; because of all the degradation and alteration, unlike interdependent economic regions, they need them.

Biology:
Interdependent vs. Independent Systems

The biological diversity of an interdependent economy should not be severely altered. Many times prey animals or herd animals of hunter-gatherer and procuring pastoral societies are purposely procured *below* an optimal amount.[49] This gives the prey population a buffer zone, so that its population remains healthy.

In more difficult times, (i.e. in times of drought or natural disaster), the maintenance of a healthy prey population pays off for the interdependent economist. The buffer zone may stave off the complete annihilation of the prey species, saving a few animals that otherwise would have died in the drought or disaster. So abundance in numbers is important for the hunter/fisher-gatherer. Both procuring pastoralists and hunter-gatherers will utilize this technique of purposeful *under*procurement.

Therefore, the biological variables of the interdependent economic system will be characterized by, high biodiversity (insured by taboos on certain species)[50] and abundance in numbers (insured by underprocurement) for non-human species.

Independent economies will tend to over-exploit the resources of the environment. The occurrence of endangered species is common in independent economies due to unfettered exploitation of resources.

Overall numbers within species also may decrease when incorporated into an independent economy. According to maximization for production, forego-

---

49. Leakey & Lewin, p. 106.
50. Leakey & Lewin, p. 98.

ing numbers in herd size for breeding of larger animals is common. Using this strategy creates a more vulnerable situation for the pastoralist in times of drought. Where interdependent pastoralism utilizes underprocurement, production pastoralism utilizes maxproduction. So, a decrease in biodiversity within the region and abundance within individual species is typical of independent economies.

The third variable under biological environment is the presence or absence of domesticated species. In interdependent systems, there is little to no domestication of species. The only domestication may be towards a species that can aid in procuring another species. This is an interdependent relationship in itself, because both the hunter and the domesticated mutually benefit from the procurement.

However, in an independent economy, the domesticated species usually *gets eaten*. It is no longer a mutually beneficial relationship, but a subjugatory one. For the domesticated species is *used* by the farmer to *serve* his needs. The domesticated species is *robbed* of the independence to obtain its own subsistence. It is made dependent upon the farmer for its subsistence.

Domestication can be of plant species as well. Agriculture is the controlled growth and consumption of domesticated species of plants. These species also are mugged of their freedom to grow by self-determination.

Subjugation of other humans can also be considered a kind of domestication. For slavery was and is prevalent in many independent economies. This time it is the people, *our own species*, that are robbed of their freedom to obtain subsistence/provisioning by self-determination.

Culture Samples

The Saami: Reindeer Herders of Northern Europe

The location is Northern Europe in the circumpolar regions of the nations of Sweden, Norway, Finland, and the Kola Peninsula of Russia. The Saami, before modernization, represent the interdependent/procuring type of pastoralism. They roamed with their reindeer herd through the toughest of weather.

The information on the Saami was found mostly in Robert Paine's 1994 book, <u>Herds of the Tundra: A Portrait of Saami Reindeer Pastoralism</u>. He actively followed a Saami herder, Ellon Ailu, his family, and reindeer in the years 1961-62.[51] This field study provided an excellent ethnographic analysis of Saami social relations, environmental conditions, and their relations with the reindeer. There was rarely a need to look elsewhere in order to find valuable data. The following represents the information I found relevant and important for this book.

At first, the Saami were hunters of the wild reindeer. But about three to four hundred years ago, some of the animals were partially "tamed". The experience and knowledge of the reindeer hunter was directly transferred to the reindeer pastoralist. The Saami used every aspect of the reindeer from food to clothing. Milching was just as important as slaughter for meat; and these were no more important than the hides. As the twentieth century ushered in the market system, meat production alone was more important than any other use. Clearly we have our first instance of the interdependence of the traditional Saami contrasted with an independent production of the twentieth century Saami.

---

51. Paine, Robert, p. 3.

Notice the thing that changes is the character of behavior towards the reindeer. The traditional subsistence technique was interdependent and procuring because every part of the reindeer was utilized. On the other hand, the twentieth century technique was characterized as independent production because only one aspect was important to the market—meat. There was a change in behavior, from interdependent/procuring to independent production, caused by the change in economy. With the change in behavior comes changes in the environment. The change to an independent/producing subsistence technique can, and in most instances does, harm the natural environment of the region.

The Saami, before exposure to modern economies, practiced reindeer herding that was primarily interdependent in nature. The reindeer herder and the reindeer themselves formed a symbiotic relationship whereby both enjoyed the benefits of sustainability and protection. The herder would make schedules that would take into account the *needs* of the animals and the animals would adapt their behavior to the schedule.[52] Paine goes on to say "the herder wishes to work *with* the herd, even as he tries to exert his will over its movements."[53] This further exemplifies the interdependent relationship the Saami have with their primary resource from the environment.

The control of animals is extremely flexible. It is the only adaptable manner in which the Saami can survive as a people. Ownership is usually done by ear-marking, but if "your" reindeer happens to flee your control, a fellow Saami will look after them until you can regain control. This promotes interdependence within the Saami family, extended family, clan, and the whole Saami people.

With independent husbandry vs. the herding of interdependent pastoralism, decisions are no longer made in a communal effort. They are made by the owner of the herd, and are usually long-term and irreversible, whereas herders, in general, make decisions that are spontaneous, short-term and pragmatic. The whole Saami people are responsible for each others' reindeer. This breeds cooperation and socio-emotional bonds between the members of the group. Whereas, with the independent Saami pastoralists, borders are built and cooperation and emotional bonds between families decrease.

---

52. Paine, p. 14.
53. Ibid., p. 15.

As mentioned above, the social environment of the Saami benefits emotionally, spiritually, and physically from the naturally interdependent pastoral economy. The coordination required in the corralling, roaming, and herding of the animals makes it mandatory for cooperation to exist not only within the family unit, but beyond, into the whole Saami people.

In addition to the social and emotional health of a Saami environment, their physical health (not totally unrelated to their social and emotional health) is also in good condition. The pressures and stresses of continuous migration in a cold and inhospitable environment made for a strong and durable physique. Also, the relatively unpolluted (unless polluted by outside cultures, i.e. Russia's Chernobyl) environment makes for healthy lungs and heart.

Within such a culture, social emotions must be high. Without others, "your" reindeer, essentially your livelihood, would be lost. In fact, the Saami show great respect for each other as manifested in their listening ability. Every time herders return from a herding excursion, they recount their story, and the whole group listens, intently. Even if the story is told before the herder arrives, the members of the group will listen to any variations and/or contradictions there might be.[54]

This is not done merely for respect and affectionate reasons. The Saami lifestyle and economic system require such detailed attention for optimal knowledge of their herd animals and the local environment. "Any discrepancies between accounts would then be weighed (to see what technique is most beneficial)."[55] So, here we observe that the emotional bonds are formed by the inherent necessity of *interdependent* pastoralism.

The shift from sled pastoralism to mechanized pastoralism causes yet another detrimental social effect. With the mechanization of pastoralism, there began a decrease in specific knowledge of the reindeer.[56] The children no longer know the intricacies of the herd and overnight stops with neighborhood Saami drop. The community and the interdependent knowledge of the reindeer population suffer. Formal schooling can not teach what the socialization of a young child in the field can teach.[57]

---

54. Taken from Paine's observation of herders after coming from an expedition.
55. Paine, p. 5.
56. Ibid., p. 148.
57. Ibid., p. 149.

In addition, since pastoral production has taken a foothold in the Saami economy, slaughter of animals for meat only has increased. From 1976 to 1985, there was a 50% increase in the number of reindeer slaughtered—from 38,000 to 70,000.[58]

Ellon Ailu, a Saami pastoralist, reluctantly sells a dozen of his reindeer to the market—whole. Upon returning home, his wife asks, "Where's the tallow? The blood? The intestinal lining? The heart? The tongue? The head? And the marrow bones?" And, "Where are the skins (for the clothing we all wear)? And, the sinew (for the sewing of that clothing)?"[59]

She obviously knew that the market would only seek-out the meat from the dozen reindeer sold, due to a high market value on reindeer meat, under an independent/production economy. She, on the other hand, had a value on *all* parts of the reindeer, in her interdependent/procuring economy. She wanted to utilize *every* part of the reindeer, wasting none of it. This is how the demands of the economic system can produce either *exploitive or non-wasteful* actions towards the environment.

The Micmac of the Eastern Woodlands

Before the 1900's and for centuries, the Micmac were hunter-gatherer-fishers of the maritime provinces of eastern Canada (i.e. Nova Scotia, New Brunswick, Prince Edward Island, Cape Breton Island, and, the Gaspé Peninsula). They traveled by birch canoes down woodland streams hunting moose, deer, caribou, bear and other lesser game.[60] They supplemented their diet with cod, eel, clams, oysters, lobster, smelt, salmon and trout.[61] In the summer, seal hunting and sea fish were a welcome treat.

Being hunter-gatherers, they also gathered wild berries and potatoes.[62] Strawberries, blueberries, raspberries and cranberries were sure to provide a sweet supplement in this naturally bountiful region. No traditional agriculture

---

58. Ibid., p. 163.
59. Paine, p. 131.
60. Wallis, Wilson D. and Ruth S., The Micmac Indians of Eastern Canada, pp. 34-42.
61. Hoffman, Bernard G., "The Historical Ethnography of the Micmac of the Sixteenth and Seventeenth Centuries", p. 127.
62. Gonzalez, Ellice B., Changing Economic Roles for Micmac Men and Women, p. 21.

was practiced because the "corn-line" is to the west, along the St. Lawrence Seaway and to the south, in New England.[63] However, there was inter-tribal trade with the Armouchiquois (of present-day Maine). They traded corn for the Micmac's extravagant jewelry items, and, fur and skin coats.

In keeping with the general rule of a 4-year birth-interval between off-spring[64], Micmac children were "rarely spaced less than two years apart, and were often nursed for three years."[65] This regulation of population growth is characteristic of hunter-gatherer societies. The economic system of hunting and gathering did not allow Micmac women the luxury of more than one child in a 4-year period.

As Leakey explains about the !Kung, also a hunting and gathering culture, "it is simply *not practical* to have more than one child bundled up in the roots and shoots of the kaross (a large leather bag slung over the shoulder to carry food and baby)."[66] This is an example of how having an interdependent econ-omy can constrain the population. A woman does not determine the number of children she has, nature does.

This natural constraint of a gathering economy is usually lifted when full pastoralism, agriculture and/or industrialism is practiced. Thus, the popula-tion increases to the extent that *people* and *their* innovations can provide the means of survival vs. what *nature* could provide by gathering. The economic system (the independent variable) is the key in determining how the popula-tion size (a dependent variable) is characterized.

The political structure of the Micmac also adheres to the general egalitarian nature of hunting/gathering societies. When there is status, it is often achieved, by either hunting skills or strength rather than inherited position.[67] In pre-colonial times, when a "leader", or sagamore (chief), is recommending a course of action, the group must give their consent or recommend a different suggestion. In this way, every person has an equal right to speak his/her mind, thereby increasing the chances that a correct or at least consensual decision is made.

In addition, the sagamore leads by *example*, rather than by *command*. It was probably not unlikely for him to lead the warriors in times of battle. How dif-

---

63. Ibid., p. 16.
64. Leakey & Lewin, p. 107.
65. Gonzales, p. 15.
66. Leakey & Lewin, p. 107.
67. Gonzales, p. 14.

ferent it is in an industrialized nation-state. The President or other executive leader is protected by servicemen and/or bodyguards. He might be arrested or taken into protective custody, if he attempted to fight in a war.

Reciprocity and food sharing, commonplace in early hunter-gatherer societies[68], were also prevalent among the Micmac. In fact, young boys who return home with their first kill are instructed to give it to others. This reinforces at an early age the need to share. Even though the environment was naturally abundant with food resources, the Micmac were still dependent on the collaboration of all the members of the band.[69]

They relied on each other for cooperation in hunting and undoubtedly in times of inter-tribal warfare, which was quite common. This mutual reliance of the Micmac probably established what I call socio-emotional bonds. They made every effort not to offend each other, so the practice of self-discipline became firmly established. If conflict did occur, within the group, it was rarely injurious in nature.

Not only did the Micmac have socio-emotional bonds between the members of their group, they had a deep spiritual respect for animals and other natural forces. Leslie F. S. Upton writes in his 1979 book, <u>Micmacs and Colonists</u>, "The respect shown to the spirits of animals ensured that the Micmacs killed only what they needed for food and clothing."[70]

This is an ideal example of interdependent procurement. Only what was *necessary* for human survival was to be procured from the environment. Additionally, all of what was taken was utilized to the fullest. There were no pollutive or wasteful practices, for fear of offending the spirits.[71]

By taking only what was *necessary* and utilizing *all* aspects of their kill, the Micmac really define what is meant by an interdependent ideology and value system. It is a value system based not on *how much can be produced* beyond what nature allows or of surplus, but of what is *necessary* only for survival.

This is the essential difference between a (surplus/producing) market economy and (subsistence/procuring) hunting-gathering economy that creates the difference in environmental ecology. In the market economy, wasteful practices are more common, thereby creating pollution to the environment. While

---

68. Leakey & Lewin, p. 137.
69. Upton, Leslie F. S., <u>Micmacs and Colonists</u>, p. 6.
70. Upton, Leslie, p. 15.
71. Ibid.

in the hunting-gathering economy, there are little, if any, wasteful practices, thereby establishing and maintaining an environment free from pollution.

The social environment of the Micmac, from the *needed* interdependence and cooperation of a hunting-gathering economy, is relatively conflict-free. Although the social bonds between the members of their group are somewhat more cognitive than emotional (i.e. by practicing self-restraint, an inherently antagonistic disposition towards others), it still indicated the need to maintain cooperation for organized hunting and protection from other neighboring tribes.[72] On the other hand, strong emotional bonds towards other species of the environment tell of their great dependence on the natural environment and the importance of maintaining deep spiritual/biological bonds with its creatures.

The fact that there seems to be stronger bonds between the Micmac and other species than between the Micmac themselves may be a function of the abundant environment. The Micmac can afford to live more independently from other Micmac, in so far as they can procure without the help of others. However, in times of scarcity, or when cooperative hunting is needed, the Micmac rule of self-restraint can come in handy by maintaining the necessary social bonds (albeit cognitive) for cooperative hunting. So the Micmac represent *a kind of independent hunting-fishing-gathering* culture. Although there is an independent tendency (e.g. increased territoriality, presumably due to fixed, predictable, and abundant recourses), the Micmac are still *primarily interdependent* in practice and ideology.

The Mohave of the Colorado

The Mohave are Native American Indians who lived along the Colorado River. They practiced simple agriculture on the naturally fertile silt deposits along both sides of the river.[73] Each spring the river would overflow its banks, leaving silt deposits and fertile well-watered ground for the Mohave. The regular deposit of rich silt each year made it unnecessary to rotate crops or to use fertilizer. The technology utilized was so simple—a planting stick with a wedge-shaped point and a slightly-curved, wooden weed cutter.[74]

---

72. Upton, Leslie, p. 3 & 19.
73. Kroeber, A. L., <u>Mohave Indians</u>, p. 25.
74. Castetter, Edward F. and Willis H. Bell, <u>Yuman Indian Agriculture</u>, pp. 94-96.

In addition to agriculture, fishing provided supplemental animal protein, along with hunting deer, rabbits, and other animals.[75] They also gathered beans, seeds, and fruits, showing that agriculture was not the sole provider of their subsistence.[76] This fact adds support to the proposition that the Mohave seem more *interdependent* than independent in some areas of their culture, even though they practiced an *independent subsistence technique*—agriculture.

The political structure was a bit more hierarchical than the Micmac hunter-gatherers. *Unlike the Micmac,* the head Mohave chief *inherited* his position, patrilineally. However, *like the Micmac,* he exerted little authority.

The Mohave territory consisted of three regional groups, which were then composed of local groups.[77] Clans existed, and their names have been documented, but their existence was more symbolic than functional.[78] Here, it is apparent that even though they practiced agriculture, hierarchy and independent ideology and behavior was *not* predominant.

Another practice that suggests egalitarianism and a more interdependent social behavior is the burning of all the deceased's belongings.[79] So, no individual family or tribe could accumulate more wealth than another. Thus, inheritance seems to be a moot point, when the items to be *inherited* (i.e. property, goods, food, and equipment) were destroyed.[80] Some funerals would completely impoverish individual families, further accentuating the value of egalitarianism.[81]

Factors that did suggest an independent ideology were: 1) the mention of disputes over property boundary markers, although, once again, like the Micmac, their *disputes* were *settled* rather *interdependently* by shoving and pushing matches,[82] and 2) their belief in Mastamho, a deity that changed into a non-deity fish-eagle. Otherwise, few other supernaturals existed, and those that did were *not* worshipped or the object of prayer,[83] suggesting relatively little con-

75. Castetter and Bell, p. 70.
76. Ibid., p. 66.
77. Stewart, Kenneth M., "Mohave." In *Handbook of North American Indians*, Vol. 10, p. 62.
78. Sherer, Lorraine M., <u>The Clan System of the Fort Mohave Indians</u>, p. 13.
79. Castetter and Bell, p. 251.
80. Ibid.
81. Castetter and Bell, p. 252.
82. Stewart, p. 58.
83. Ibid., pp. 65-66.

cern with maintaining a biological or spiritual bond with creatures or forces of the environment. Also, nuclear families were the basic social and economic unit, suggesting *self-sufficiency*, although members of the extended family at times aided in farming duties.[84]

All in all, the Mohave represent a mix of interdependent and independent philosophy and behavior. This may not be a refutation of my theory; rather, it is a great example of how interdependent and independent subsistence techniques co-existing in one culture can exhibit and promote both independent and interdependent ideology and behavior. It actually draws support for the theory that the economic practices of a certain culture will correlate rather well with the ideology, behavior, and character of the culture.

The Nubians of Southern Egypt

The Nubians are a very peaceful people.[85] They live, like the Mohave, near a river (i.e. the Nile), which over-flows its banks each year, depositing alluvium and dampening the soil.[86] Therefore, agriculture naturally found its way into their local economy. Cultivation of quick-growing crops like millet was predominant along with the gathering of wild grasses and plants.[87] However, when the Romans introduced the water-wheel (eskalays) for irrigation, the Nubians were able to extend the area under cultivation and the duration of cultivation.[88]

The population of the Nubian valley numbered a few hundred thousand, when peaceful conditions prevailed.[89] Although this is more populous than the Mohave valley, it could not support great population centers. Therefore, Nubia remained on the periphery to myriad kingdoms.

This fact seems to go along with the theory that increasing independence in economy leads to increasing population size. The introduction of irrigation and the utilization of cattle,[90] both indicate independent behaviors and *more so* than the Mohave.

---

84. Ibid., pp. 64-65.
85. Fernea, Robert A., Nubians in Egypt, p. 17.
86. Ibid., p. 8.
87. Ibid., p. 8.
88. Ibid.
89. Ibid.
90. Fernea, p. 18.

The Mohave population numbered about 3,000 in 1770, 4,000 in 1872, and 1,050 in 1910.[91] The relatively low population of the Mohave correlates with their rather interdependent, although agricultural, local economy.[92] Whereas, the Nubian's population has reached into the hundreds of thousands. I am confident that their more sophisticated and predominantly agricultural economy, when compared to the Mohave limited agriculture, had no small hand in increasing the population size.

The political structure of the Nubians was hierarchical, and Christian churches were established.[93] In addition, cultural complexity in painting of houses (inside and outside), colored clothing, jewelry in hair and around neck and arms, and designed basket-weaving all suggest an increase in leisure and cultural complexity, which may symbolize an increased independence from natural constraints.

Trade with adjacent nation-states or kingdoms may have also added to the need for a hierarchy in Nubia. Here it seems that three factors may have influenced the political structure of the Nubians. One, the reliance on agriculture, as an economic subsistence base, creates a population large enough for hierarchy to form. Two, the introduction of irrigation and domestication of animals further expanded this population. Three, trade with neighboring states presented even more of a need to have someone (or some office) represent the wishes of the people. All of these factors increase independence from nature, thereby making them independent establishments of Nubian culture.

A look into marriage ceremonies will also provide clues to support the supposition that Nubians had an independent culture. Marriages are heavily based on shareholdings and family relationships.[94] Even before they are born, children are engaged to be married. This stress on the importance of material wealth is common in societies with production economies. In other words, societies that place importance on a man's holdings (control of property) begin to value a *man's* wealth—vs.—the *natural* wealth of a region.

By separating the economic need of the family from nature and placing it on a person, the tendency for humans to further dominate and control nature increases. People become the limited resource of the agricultural and industrial

---

91. Stewart, p. 57.
92. Recall that fishing, hunting, and gathering remained important to their subsistence.
93. Fernea, pp. 8-9.
94. Fernea, p. 27.

society. The more efficiently they exploit the environment, the more they are worth. This sets off an aggressive behavior in (and competition among) males that, I would argue, has never been witnessed in all of history.

The hierarchical nature of Nubian society, also demonstrates a dominating viewpoint of humans over nature. Not only do humans see themselves above other species, but they also see themselves over others of their kind! Thus, we begin to see slavery and subjugated classes of people in agricultural societies. In fact, the Nubians themselves were traded as slaves for food, horses, and cloth to the Egyptians.[95] They were also utilized by other (adjacent) kingdoms as a tributary (peripheral) source of income.[96]

The Taiwanese

The newly industrialized nation of Taiwan was formerly a tributary of China and Japan, economically. Taiwan provided much of the agricultural product for China and Japan, while meagerly subsiding on the left-overs.[97]

Now, as an industrialized nation, Taiwan is left on the periphery of the core nations of China, Japan and other Western developed nations. Although it is part of the world economy of capitalism, it is on periphery-end of the capitalist stick. The core nations use these peripheral, newly "independent" nation-states as their resource base. The elite nations no longer have to subjugate their own people, but subjugate *other people of other nations.*[98]

Now that the population of Taiwan is enculturated to the European economic system, the environment will be exploited to an even greater degree. The previous system of agriculture, albeit an independent step from nature, was at least sustainable. But continuous deforestation, pollution, and population growth present serious dilemmas for the Taiwanese.

Similarly, many other "independent" nation-states will have these consequences to their physical, social, and biological environment. That is why it is important to understand the dynamics of culture and how the adoption of an economic system is key in determining the ideology, behavior, and subsequent effects on local, regional, and global environments. The kind of economic sys-

---

95. Fernea, p. 9.
96. Ibid., p. 8.
97. Li, Dr. K. T., <u>Economic Transformation of Taiwan</u>, p. 6.
98. Giddens, Anthony, <u>The Consequences of Modernity</u>, pp. 70-71.

tem that the culture adopts is critical to determining what kind of physical, social and biological environments it will produce.

Many of the aboriginal peoples of Taiwan have been incorporated into this industrial economy.[99] Of the Ami and the Puyuma of the Eastern Lowlands, the Saisiat of the Western Lowlands, and the Central Mountain Groups of Paiwan-Rukai, Bunun, Tsou, and Atayal, nearly all have been adopted into the modernized agricultural and industrial economy. The others have been driven into the mountains.[100]

Before induction, these people hunted, fished, gathered, and practiced horticulture.[101] Their mode of subsistence was *basically* interdependent with their environment. No major deforestation or other massive alterations to the environment were performed before the introduction of labor-intensive agriculture and/or industrialization. These new subsistence techniques, undoubtedly, destroyed much of the biological and physical environments of Taiwan, but also caused social discord as well.

Introduction into the big cities and villages of industry must have been a stressful change culturally, since nuclear homes, hamlets and villages of no more than 1000 people at maximum were the norm for these people.[102] Among the Ami, fighting between tribes was quite frequent, owing to a relatively large population of about 52,000 in 1939, on a relatively small island. In 1975, their population had risen to 90,000, most likely due to the expansion and intensification of the economic system. The western coastal plain holds nearly 98 percent of Taiwan's population, amounting to over 2,700 people per square mile.[103] Nearly every bit of tillable land has been sectioned and is under cultivation.[104]

Over the past forty years, Taiwan has averaged an annual real economic growth rate of 8 percent, one of the highest in the world. This could not have been done if industrialism was not so adamantly pursued by Sun Yat-sen.[105]

---

99. LeBar, Frank M., "Part IV. Formosa." *Ethnic Groups of Insular Southeast Asia*, Vol. 2, p. 116.
100. LeBar, p. 116.
101. Chang, Kwang-Chih, Fengpitou, Tapenkeng, and the Prehistory of Taiwan, pp. 64-79.
102. LeBar, p. 130.
103. LeBar, Frank M., p. 116.
104. Wolf, Margery, The House of Lim, p. 3.
105. Gregor, A. James, Ideology and Development: Sun Yat-sen and the Economic History of Taiwan, p. 2.

Sun Yat-sen believed that China could only compete globally if it protected its region militarily and economically by adopting a program of agricultural modernization, industrialization, and "equitable" income distribution.[106] This equitable distribution was in fact one of the most impressive features of the industrial development of China and the province of China—Taiwan.

According to the land-to-the-tiller legislation, the tillers of the soil became the private owners of the soil. This not only increased incentive to produce more (because the more you produce, the more money you make), but also distributed the wealth more or less *equally* among the population.[107]

Normally, wealth created by the market system accumulates in the hands of the few, whereas in Taiwan, the ratio of the distribution of wealth between the top 20% and the bottom 20% in 1979 was 4.3.[108] Japan, Sweden, and Sri Lanka were close seconds, with 5.2, 5.6, and 5.8, respectively. This showed how socially the increase in material wealth of an industrial economy does not have to concentrate in the hands of the few.

Another reason why Taiwan was such an industrial success was its reliance on developing agriculture first.[109] Instead of just skipping right into industrial production, agriculture, which had already been practiced small-scale, was stepped-up and mechanized so that productivity and surplus increased.[110] This then could be exported to other nations. The revenue from the agricultural exports could then be used to invest in heavy industry.[111] After industry was established, self-dependence could begin, and, a rare occurrence among newly industrializing nations in the international market, Taiwan became economically self-reliant.[112]

---

106. Ibid., p. 11.
107. Ibid., p. 31.
108. Li, Dr. K. T., p. 57.
109. Ibid., p. 42.
110. Ibid., p. 43.
111. Ibid., p. 44.
112. Ibid., p. 58.

Analysis

The economic systems that we have analyzed in this report have been rather more mixed than clearly defined. Messy, the way real systems tend to be, especially when analyzed anthropologically.

Although there were mixed economies, the correlational characteristics of the environments under study followed the general theoretical proposition that independent economic systems will tend to correspond with: 1) low socio-emotional bonds within the human population and among other species, 2) high levels of alteration and manipulation of the environment, 3) low biodiversity and numbers, 4) high population growth and pollutive practices, 5) inherited or established hierarchical political structure, 6) the presence of private property, and 7) domesticated species.

On the other hand, interdependent economic systems correlate with: 1) high biodiversity and numbers, 2) low levels of alteration and/or manipulation of the physical *and* biological environment (i.e. domestication of animals), 3) high levels of bonding between and within species, 4) moderate-low population growth, 5) no pollutive practices, 6) achieved hierarchy or egalitarian socio-political structure, and 7) sharing of resources.

Independent economic systems, (i.e. agriculture, production pastoralism, and industry), produce social conditions that are low in emotional bonds, (not only between species and the environment, but between each other) due to the liberation of the biological need to depend on each other for subsistence. By adopting an independent subsistence economy and ideology, people's behavior starts to change from an affectionate and interdependent disposition to an unaffectionate and independent disposition.

According to Sahlins, the greater the kinship or social distance is between people, the less likely that the persons involved will give *without* expectation of return, a.k.a. *generalized reciprocity*.[113] Kin relatives are given food, clothing, and any other material needed unconditionally with *no expectation of return*, while trade with members of other tribes is often *negotiated* to gain an *edge* in the exchange, a.k.a. *negative reciprocity*. In the middle of the kin/social-distance continuum, balanced reciprocity is the norm. Here, it is customary to expect some *approximate equivalent* in return, either immediately or in the short-term.[114]

With the introduction of an independent economy, the zone in which emotional and generalized *reciprocity* is practiced, *shrinks*. Food, which is generally *not bought and/or traded* for things in interdependent economies, *can be and is* bought or traded, as a rule.[115] This is a good example of how the essentially *social-affinal exchange* of food in traditional cultures has turned into an *asocial-inimical exchange* of food (as a commodity) in modern-day cultures.

Independent cultures also correlate with detrimental physical conditions of the environment. Soil erosion, deforestation, pollution, and depletion of resources are part of the environmental devastation of the twentieth century.

The biological conditions of independent/producing cultures are also left to suffer. Decreasing biodiversity, indicated by endangered species of plants and animals, and low numbers within these species, are all too common in an industrializing world. Should newly forming nation-states adopt an economy that continuously produces these kinds of conditions?

Saami of Northern Europe

The Saami represent an excellent case study for analyzing the affects that different economic systems have on social, physical and biological environments of an indigenous people. Before the introduction of production pastoralism, the Saami pastoralist worked interdependently with the reindeer herd. The herder listened to the needs of the reindeer, and the reindeer responded by reforming their movements to the herder's request.[116] This interdependence led to stable population numbers within the reindeer herd. Therefore, the reindeer's abundance in numbers was *not significantly affected* under the interdependent economic system, transhumance.

---

113. Sahlins, Marshall, <u>Stone Age Economics</u>, p. 191.
114. Ibid., p. 195.
115. Ibid., p. 216.
116. Paine, Robert, p. 15.

On the other hand, when full pastoralism was introduced, it was more con-ducive to the meat market to grow larger, more sedentary animals. This put more emphasis on larger reindeer, which led to a decrease in reindeer popula-tion and an increase in the number of fat reindeer. Lean reindeer became an anomaly for the Saami. This no doubt affected the physical health of the Saami by increases in fat intake. This along with the increased sedentary nature of production pastoralism (as I have termed it), also can contribute to deleterious health effects.

The biodiversity of the Saami region must also have decreased with the increased breeding of domesticated reindeer for meat production. Wolves and other predators are almost extinct in these regions (unless domesticated for Saami use), due to the decrease in available prey.[117] Saami protect their rein-deer from wild animals, so that their numbers *un*naturally increase.

Before pastoralism for production, the Saami would utilize every part of the reindeer. Now, they sell them to the market, and buy clothing, sewing materi-als, etc., which would have all been provided by the reindeer. The social envi-ronment under a market economy is different from the social environment of the pastoral economy of old times. The children are sent away to learn new things in schools that the market economy requires them to learn.[118] The chil-dren are taught a more generalized education (about the world and their place in it) versus the more specialized and skill-specific training they received when taught at home or in the field. This changes their perception of the world and their relationship to their parents. No longer does the child receive the special-ized and personal attention from its parents and kin that is inherently coordi-nated with such specialized and skill-specific training.

The knowledge that the Saami attained about their reindeer herds can only be gained through a mutual concern for survival between the two species. An intimate bond is created, which in turn creates a biological connection between the two species. When the system under which the two species oper-ate changes its disposition to a-matter-of-(mere)economics, there ceases to exist an emotional connection. The biological bond still exists, because, after all, the Saami still *rely on the reindeer*, only this time *as a commodity* for market. However, *the emotional connection* is diminished by the mitigation of *the Saami reliance* on *the intrinsic (use) value* of the reindeer, which is caused by the incor-

---

117. Beach, Hugh, p. 228.
118. Gellner, Ernest, <u>Nations And Nationalism</u>, p. 38.

poration into a market economy. Consequently, reindeer and Saami may *not really* know each other for much longer *as they once did* when they lived harmoniously and interdependently together. Often it takes *true intimacy* to really gain adequate knowledge of things.[119] With the loss of the ability to gain true insight through intimacy, will the Saami people lose this ancient bond of life with their reindeer?

The Micmac

The Micmac represent the next culture that, hypothetically, represents an interdependent economy, and the social, physical and biological environments characteristic of such an economy.

Now, that most of the Micmac have been incorporated into a market economy as lumberjacks, farmers or other workers, their population is on the rise. In 1972, the population was 9,805.[120] This represents 6,305 more people (from 3,500 to 9,805) in the same geographic region. This increase in population coincides with a gradual change in the subsistence pattern from hunting and gathering, in the 17th to 19th centuries, to cultivation in the late 19th century, and later, to industrialization in 20th century.

Another "coincidence" with the meeting of Europeans happens to be the dramatic depletion of "fur-bearing" animals, i.e. wolves, bear, and caribou. Instead of hunting these species for *food procurement* only, the Micmac began hunting to produce a *supply* of fur for the fur-trade, popular in the 1800s. Consequently, biodiversity was threatened by extinction of species, and numbers were dwindling, creating endangered species.[121] Where once there was a naturally abundant environment the fur-trade market system effectively decreased abundance and diversity.

The social environment of the Micmac also changed with the change in subsistence pattern. In the old ways, one would do whatever it took *not* to insult someone else or otherwise cause conflict within the group. This is characteristic of a social group whose members literally and biologically *depend* on each other for survival. Food sharing, collaborative hunting, and coherence of

---

119. Jagger, Alison, <u>Love and Knowledge: Emotion in Feminist Epistemology</u>, p. 162.

120. Bock, Philip K., "Micmac." In *Handbook of North American Indians,* Vol. 15, p. 120.

121. Hoffman, p. 124.

force against neighboring tribes all represent a need to put aside personal differences for the betterment of the group.

The modern day Micmac people, although still remaining respectful of their past culture, operate under a very different economic system. One that *strives* on individual freedom and effort. This individual freedom is expanding, so it seems, while the Micmac as a whole are broken apart. The extended family, which was integral to early Micmac society, has given way to the nuclear family.[122] "Individualized wage labor efforts served to reinforce the nuclear family rather than a large kin group as the economic unit."[123] In addition, the division of labor between men and women began to favor men. Lumberjacking, fishing, and hunting all provided economic means of survival through monetary income for the late 19th and 20th century Micmac. With this came the devaluation of Micmac women within the household.[124] Although they provided extraneous income through selling baskets and gathering wild berries, women were not a primary source of income for survival.

The Mohave and Nubians

The Mohave continued to collect beans, seeds, and fruits. Even though they planted beans, it is remarkable that they sustained part of the interdependent lifestyle in gathering beans. They also hunted deer, rabbits, and other animals as well as fished.[125] This makes them more interdependent than the Nubians, who used complex mechanization and domesticated animals.[126]

However, the Mohave were a bit more independent than the Micmac. As expected, the Micmac hunter-gatherers are more interdependent than the Mohave agriculturists, just by virtue of their economic system. In the former, people are totally interdependent and procuring in nature, and in the latter, men or women begin to alter the productivity of the environment by *purposely* planting seeds nearby the river. We see a gradient starting to form between the Micmac, the Mohave, and the Nubians.

The Nubians represent among the agriculturists the more independent and producing economy. The Mohave, the other agriculturist group, represent a

---

122. Gonzales, p. 94.
123. Gonzales, p. 94.
124. Ibid., p. 95.
125. Castetter and Bell, pp. 179 & 211.
126. Fernea, frame #21.

more *interdependent* economic system. And the Micmac, being *strictly* hunter, fisher-gatherers, represent the most interdependent and *procuring* economic system. The below diagram illustrates what we have discovered thus far:

Hunter-Gatherers   Agriculturists

_____

Micmac   Mohave   Nubians

Diagram 1

The Mohave, in the middle of the diagram, are agriculturists, which skews them independently. However, they still practiced hunting, gathering, and fishing, which skews them *interdependently*. Therefore, they represent a mixed economy of interdependence and independence.

The Mohave are interdependent because they *still* gathered beans, while planting them nearby the river. Additionally, they used no fertilizers and/or animal domestication, as did the Nubians. They are independent to the extent that they are agriculturists. By definition, planting seed or doing anything else that *actively* produces more from the environment than what grows *naturally*, they represent an independent culture.

As an addendum to diagram 1, we must not forget about the traditional Saami and market Saami, whom should be placed as follows:

Transhumant Pastoralists   Full Pastoralists
Hunter-Gatherers   Agriculturists

_____

Micmac   Mohave   Nubians
Traditional Saami   Market Saami

Diagram 2

The Saami of tradition are categorized as very *interdependent*, along with the Micmac.

The Saami, after participation in the market, become more *independent* by enlarging reindeer size, settling down in permanent settlements, and selling reindeer to the market *merely* for their meat. In this manner, the Saami become more like the Nubians with their independent behaviors of animal domestication, mechanization, and irrigation.

- Note: Even the Micmac, the most interdependent culture analyzed, when incorporated into the market system by fur-trade, became more *independent* in nature. So it seems that trade between groups results in creating a surplus by: 1) in the case of agriculturists, growing additional agricultural produce for sale in market, 2) in the case of pastoralists, breeding larger animals, or 3) in the case of hunter-gatherers, procuring from nature a *supply*, beyond a subsistence-level, of a *market-valued* species.

Market Saami

The Saami pastoralist became sedentary after introduction into the market system.[127] The herders became husbanders,[128] marking the beginning of the end of the interdependent Saami. In the traditional household, men, women, and children were all expected to help with the herd of reindeer.[129] They lived in mobile tents, or *lavvos*, like the Micmac wigwam.[130] With the incorporation into the market economy, they began to live on permanent settlements. With this comes the over-grazing of land, the stockcading of reindeer, and conflict over ownership of lands.[131] The Saami husbander presents more of an intrusion on nature than does the Saami herder. Modern Saami behavior is independent in nature, thus breaking the bonds of interdependence between man and reindeer.

---

127. Paine, p. 143.
128. Beach, p. 36.
129. Paine, p. 103.
130. Ibid., p. 45.
131. Ibid., pp. 154 & 159.

A Micmac Exception

The Micmac were labeled as the most interdependent culture analyzed, and for the most part, that is accurate. However, I would like to suggest a possible exception to their seemingly benign interdependence.

Their environment was particularly abundant with species, and their values to utilize all of their kill and to kill *only* what was necessary, maintained this biodiversity and abundance. This consequently created strong bonds between them and other species.

However, the bonds among the members of the group seemed more cognitive than emotional. The fact that they had to restrain themselves from acting aggressively towards one another suggests that their need for each other's survival was somewhat limited.

Perhaps the overall abundance in their physical environment provided enough slack to loosen the bonds between members of the group. In such an environment, hunters will be more successful, more often, and the need for reciprocity may diminish. In scarcely resourced environments, the need for reciprocity may be greater, thereby producing greater emotive/biological bonding among group members.

The Taiwanese

The island of Taiwan represents a case of an intense agricultural economy, which gradually turns into the most progressive industrial economy of recent history.[132] The Taiwanese, made up of indigenous peoples, Han Chinese, and other Asian peoples, have all come together under one ideology of development. Consequently, this minute island is one of the most populated places on the planet. Intense agriculture and industry have really out-done themselves when we analyze how population size in Taiwan has increased with respect to these independent economies.

Before industrial and agricultural production, the population of Taiwan was only in the thousands.[133] By the mid-1960's, the Chinese population of Taiwan was 13 million.[134] This prompted the Taiwan government to implement a population regulation policy and to adopt family

---

132. Li, Dr. K. T., p. 13.
133. LeBar, p. 116.
134. Ibid.

planning.[135] Birth control and the renunciation of the popular proverb that, "having many sons and many grandsons was a blessing," represented steps that were taken to help control the burgeoning population.[136]

In keeping with the problems of intense agricultural production, the physical environment of Taiwan must have been irrevocably altered. In fact, the name "Taiwan" means terraced bay,[137] which the Chinese gave the island.

The economic base to compete in the world-wide market was founded on: 1) developing an agricultural economy, 2) using agricultural production for trade and subsistence, and 3) using the profits from trade to establish an industrial economy.[138] It "fortunately" worked very well for the new industrial Taiwan, but *unfortunately* it severely changed the landscape of the island.

The biology of the island must also have suffered. With an incredible increase in human population, massive reclamation of land over to agricultural use, and the establishment of heavy industry, the biodiversity of species on this sub-tropical island assuredly suffered. These deleterious environmental effects are all over-shadowed by the supposed light of material economic progress. Taiwan has been proclaimed an inspiration, even a "model", to other developing industrial nations.[139] It surely has developed a successful subsistence economy for the human species in the region. Meanwhile, the rest of the species of the island seem to be disappearing for lack of living space.

So then, to the extent that an industrial economy is successful within a region, the rest of the environment can be said to lose its ability to maintain its "economy". This is due to the inherently independent disposition of modern economic systems. They do not allow for, or factor in, the economies of other species. On the other hand, this is what an interdependent system *does* do. By disposing the self as an integral part of the whole, the economies of each species fit together nicely, to create a well-functioning, sustainable, and interdependent economy of life.

This economy of life includes human economic systems, as long as they remain connected and interdependent with the economies of other species. When people diverge from the economy of the system by posing themselves as

---

135. Li, Dr. K. T., p. 61.
136. Ibid., p. 61.
137. Copper, John F., Historical Dictionary of Taiwan, p. 101.
138. Gregor, p. 49.
139. Ibid., p. 85.

apart from nature, their economies begin to erase the economies of other species.

This "eraser effect" of other species' economies can be likened to the eraser effect that certain predominant economies have on lesser economies, e.g. economies of scale erasing subsistence economies.

Summary

Social Variables

Now let's look at the social variables for each culture.

	Trad.Saami: Herders	Market Saami	Micmac: Hunt-Gath	Mohave: Sim.Agri.	Nubians: Com.Agri.	Taiwanese: Agri.&Ind
Population	5000	35000	3500	4000	300000	13 million
Political Struct.	Egalitarian	Inheritance	Achieve	Slight Inher	Inheritance	Hierarchy
Soc.-emotions	Int.Rel.	Ext.Rel.	Int.Rel.	Pri.Ext.Rel	Ext.Rel.	Ext.Rel.
Share vs. Own	Share	Own	Share	Own	Own	Own

Now, let us take time to draw up a scale of relative interdependence or independence in relation to **social environment** for each of our culture samples.

Interdependent   Independent

———————————————————————————————————————

Micmac   Traditional Saami   Mohave   Nubians & Market Saami   Taiwanese

The first *social characteristic* is population, and is self-explanatory. The more independent the economy is, the higher the population.

The second variable is *political structure*. It ranges from egalitarian to hierarchical. The Micmac and the procuring Saami represented a relatively egali-

46

tarian society. If there was any hierarchy formed, it was only temporary and based on ability or achieved status.[140] Even here, the sagamore (chief) of the Micmac had to confer with others of the group before taking any action. The Saami herders had unwritten laws that gave the right to any man, woman, or child, to direct or control wayward reindeer.[141]

Inheritance, which implies ownership of resources, begins to appear with sedentarism in agriculture or in production pastoralism. Resources, such as land for the Mohave, land and reindeer for the Saami, and land, cattle and mechanized irrigation wheels for the Nubians, were all *owned* by individuals or their families. Ownership implies that individuals are dominant over the land, its products, and its creatures. This is typified by our last culture sample, the Taiwanese.

Industry and agriculture have permeated every part of Taiwan, even parts that are seemingly impervious to them.[142] Taiwan's economy is totally redistributive, meaning that a central government plans, regulates, and redistributes the resources of the economy. Fortunately, the land-to-the-tiller program and Sun's ideology of equal income distribution has provided the majority of the people a fair standard of living. However, there are some that fall through the cracks of this inherently exploitive economic system, which may pose a problem for China down the road.[143]

An industrial economic system goes one step further than the other economic systems, in that it has an established hierarchy in which some people are owners, while others are producers. Where the agricultural economies enslave *animals* to help produce the resources of a society, industrial economies enslave *their own* people to help produce the resources of so-called "civilized" society.

If we permit civility to mean that We are an enlightened/intelligent species and as such We ought treat each other with a higher degree of compassion and kindness (i.e. humanity), are *we* really so civilized (or humane) when we enslave our own people to do the arduous and alienating work of modern industrial society? In reality, is it true that the few, the owners, are most humane (or civilized), or do they just appear to be so? Concomitantly, are not the producers/enslaved, the ones who are often called "uncivilized" or "inhu-

---

140. Gonzales, p. 14.
141. Paine, p. 15.
142. Wolf, p 3.
143. Li, Dr. K. T., p. 142.

mane", the ones who are more "civilized" and/or "humane"? Perhaps **both** the owners *and* the producers are *desensitized/dehumanized* in an inherently insensitive and merely economical economic system.

Furthermore, is it not logical to call humane the ones who take care of other people in society, who are the workers/producers? If we take humanity to mean being concerned for others in society, then are not the ones who work nearly seven days a week, thereby showing a great deal of concern for their fellow man, the most humane?

Maybe it is the ones who *profit* off the labor of *genuinely* concerned people, who are *in*humane. For how humane, civil, or socially appropriate is it to exploit the efforts of others in society? Socially inappropriate behavior is common among individuals with emotional handicaps.[144] Perhaps the emotionally deficient economies of independent systems are the basis of the inherently-flawed social relations that exist in such societies.

I suggest that the industrial economic system and other independent systems produce an inherently *"in*humane" social polity. People are pitted against each other, creating a never-ending, perpetual competition, which in turn produces an increased surplus, which is then *exploited* by the ones who create the system. Ingenious for the few (elite), but sad for the society as a whole.

The third social characteristic analyzed is level of social emotion in the culture, which includes emotion between species. These emotions form bonds between the members of the group and other species, to the extent that they are *dependent* on each other for survival. These bonds between the members of the group and other species form from the *biological need* to depend on each other for subsistence and survival.

An interdependent economic system can foster social relations of love and respect for other members of the group. Newly-emerging nationalist sentiment (nationalism) can also foster social relations of mutual love and respect for others in a society, but this sentiment is somewhat different. The love and respect that one member of the society has for another member of the same society is based on their *mutual inclusion in that society*. It is a kind of *exclusive* love *in terms of membership in a particular society/culture* versus the more *inclusive* love of interdependent economies, which does not concern itself with belonging to any particular culture but rather with *belonging to a particular species* (and in this sense it is *exclusive*) (i.e. as long as you are human and are aid-

144. Damasio, Antonio, pp. 62-79.

ing me in the struggle for survival, then "I love you, and you are included in my love party!").

Relative informality and/or formality of religion were used to indicate level of social emotion in a culture. Formal religions tend to demonstrate morality *externally*, in places of worship and in written laws. Low-levels of social emotion correlate well with the formality of religion in a culture. The reason why these cultures establish external measures and structures of religion is because of the inherently low levels of internal religion within the society.

On the other hand, informal religion tends to be integral to the social relationships of daily life in interdependent economic systems. Emotions in society are high, and compliance is maintained by them.

The Micmac, the Saami, and the Mohave all had shamanistic beliefs which indicate that their religion was an important component in obtaining subsistence. However, in the Mohave case, we see a decrease in reliance on spiritual divinities. They believed that Mastamho was responsible for the creation of the land and *taught* the people how to live.[145] The important concept here is that *the god* bestowed upon the people *the knowledge* of how to produce their own subsistence versus the belief that *the god(s)* provide their subsistence. (*Note:* This characteristic was also prevalent in Mayan culture. They were also agriculturists, that believed *the god(s)* provided them *with knowledge* of how to grow corn.)[146]

The Nubians and Taiwanese, on the other hand, were assimilated into external religions, Islam and Catholicism, respectively. When the religion is separated out of the daily activities of procuring subsistence, it is evidence that people have lost a biological necessity to maintain an emotionally sympathetic bond between members of the human species and other species. This is where we start to see over-exploitation and significant pollution (i.e. wastefulness) in human behavior. Both the Nubians and the Taiwanese over-exploited other species.

---

145. Sherer, p. 8.
146. Tedlock, Dennis, <u>Popul Vuh</u>, p. 147.

Physical & Biological (Ecological) Variables

Now we will examine the biological and physical variables observed for each culture.

	Trad.Saami: Herders	Market Saami	Micmac: Hunt-Gath	Mohave: Sim.Agri.	Nubians: Com.Agri.	Taiwanese: Agri.&Ind.
Manipulation	Minimal	Present	Absent	Minimal	Present	Maximal
Pollution	Absent	Present	Absent	Minimal	Minimal	Present
Biodiversity	Med.: regn	Lo.: regn, domes,pop.	High: regn & pop.	Lo.: regn	Lo.: regn, domes, pop.	Lo.: pop.
Abundance	High: strategy	High: strategy	High: region	Low: region	High:strategy	High: strategy
Domestication	Slight	Full	Absent	Slight	Full	Full & Mec.

This next scale represents the relative interdependence/independence of each culture analyzed with respect to **biological and physical aspects of the environment:**

Interdependent   Independent

Micmac Mohave Traditional Saami Nubians Market Saami Taiwanese

Notice that the above **biological and physical environment scale** is *different from* the previously analyzed **social environment scale,** which is again featured below:

Interdependent   Independent

Micmac   Traditional Saami   Mohave   Nubians & Market Saami Taiwanese

Conclusion

In conclusion, the cultures analyzed conformed to general pattern and expected results. Primarily independent cultures of the market Saami, the Nubians, and the Taiwanese displayed, as expected, problematic characteristics in relation to their social, biological, and physical environments.

Predominantly interdependent cultures like the Micmac, the traditional Saami, and the Mohave, all displayed relatively non-intrusive characteristics within their respective environments. This study should be useful for so-called "developing" nation-states who are deciding on what kind of economic system is appropriate for their region. Perhaps none of the above, some of the above, or some characteristics of the above economies will be appropriate. Whichever is the best economy for the people of the region, *and* the region itself, ought be the primary objective.

WE must learn to develop an economic system that is integral to the "economic systems" of the other species of a region. To continue to live as though we are invulnerable to nature's forces and her creatures has been, and surely will continue to be, a fallacious philosophy.

Given all this, **why or how** is it possible that so-called adaptive, primitive, interdependent and sound economies are being constantly and increasingly replaced by newly emerging economies of scale which are supposed to be maladaptive and fallacious? I believe adaptability must be measured in the context of term length. Primitive interdependent economies are born in a specific region of origin and are attuned naturally and selected according to the biological, physical and social conditions of that region. These economies, by virtue of evolving from the processes of natural selection, must be **adaptive.** We do not know **how long** some of these economies have existed, but we do know that they have been around for a very long time, i.e. tens and hundreds of thousands of years.

On the other hand, modern or increasingly "independent" economies have only been around for thousands of years, beginning with the domestication of wild animals and plants. These economies, since this time, have been and continue to be supplanting the more primitive and interdependent economies of the various regions of the world. In addition, they do it without regard to the physical, biological or sociological conditions of the particular regions. This frequently leads to the disruption and degradation of newly-independent regions.

Now we should return to the question of **why and how** these newly independent economies of scale are replacing traditional interdependent subsistence economies throughout the world. First, the people of the self-sufficient regions are fascinated by the idea that they can have luxury items that otherwise would not be possible. Second, they are told that they can be relatively assured that they will have a constant food supply, and other necessities of life, if they work and secure money in various endeavors of the new economy. Many indigenes except these terms **without** realizing the potential detrimental effects to the physical and biological environment and often overlooked, the potential effects on their social and cultural environment. Their sociocultural environment that has evolved over generations is *specifically* and *adaptively* formed according to the allowances of the geographic region. As consequence of the adoption of a culture that normally would not evolve in such a region, the geographic region may be fit with a culture that does not "belong to it." Consequently, the culture and concomitant behavior has the potential to affect the region in *a negative* and *an intrusive* manner. Therefore, the intruding economies of scale are *not adaptive* towards the biological, physical and social environments of prospective regions, but *only* adaptive to the biological, physical and sociological aspects of the regions from which they originated. **Where are these places?**

To determine where humans first began to significantly increase their independence from natural dependence and/or strengthen their reliance on technology is too overwhelming a task for this book. For this book we are only concerned with **why and how** these systems are increasingly overcoming *the naturally-evolved economies of the various regions of the world.*

One of the reasons **why** modern economic systems overcome more simple interdependent economic systems is in their technological and military superiority. If the economies of primitives had technological power they would displace economies of scale, or at least be able to fend them off. But, in seeking to remain interdependent with nature, these economies never have the desire or need to develop the ability to dominate technologically, other species, nature, or each other. Increasingly independent economies, on the other hand, **do** develop a need to protect resources and **do** desire developing technologically for the purposes of increased efficiency in environmental exploitation and for the protection of the resources extracted.

Another way economies of scale have replaced subsistence economies is **by incorporating** the primitive people into a market economy; through trade or colonization. This effectively changes the culture of the people to a modern industrial culture, which affects attitudes and dispositions towards the environment. With the continual incorporation of the world's various cultures into the global industrial economy, the cultural diversity of our species is threatened. This could inevitably lead to a lack of stability in our species. Diversity is the foundation of stability.

Economies of scale replace subsistence economies because they are **immediately and individualistically** adaptive, and since most of humankind's cultures operate on an individually-oriented framework, this is successful. But, if We act in the interest of our species as a whole (thereby using a group-level strategy) independent economies will prove to be maladaptive. (Note: Interdependent economies seek to aid group (species) long-term survival). An individual level (our species, our economic system, only) disposition is not the most effective long-term survival strategy because it fails to account for the needs of other species and other cultures. WE need a strategy that allows other species and other cultures to have their specifically-adaptive economies survive without which We as a whole can not survive, in so far as these are geared toward distinct and changing geographic and climatic regions of earth. To expect all cultures to adopt one way, one culture, one economic system is dangerous and maladaptive in the long-term. Environments change, and if every culture adopts one culture that does not look to accommodate the specific needs of various geographic regions of the globe, there is danger of creating an environment which may, in the end, not even be **able to sustain human life.** We poison ourselves!

In the short-term these economies may be *successful,* but there are reasons to believe these systems are, in the long-term, maladaptive. To the extent that these systems are based on frequency-dependent behavior—i.e. where the probability for success decreases as the number of people following the strategy increases, they are short-term strategies.[147] For instance, as more people adopt the ideology of progress (an ever-increasing exploitation of the environ-

147. Barkow, Jerome H., "The Elastic Between Genes and Culture", p. 377.

ment), which originally *was* an adaptive strategy, the environment becomes over-exploited. The population either crashes, emigrates, (if there is anywhere to go), or develops alternative resource strategies, (if it's not already too late).[148]

Frequency-dependent strategies select for beneficial behavior at an individual level. Individualist cultures, such as the more independent variety, will be successful against competing interdependent cultures. Such cultures increasingly become technology-dependent, whereas interdependent cultures seek to maintain their nature-dependent strategies. A "positive" consequence of advanced technological dependence is the ability to make sophisticated weaponry, whereas interdependent cultures will not seek to develop and in many cases are not able to develop sophisticated weaponry. Therefore, they are and can be eliminated very easily through raw power. However, the duration of an independent economy's reign is limited by the time it takes for the resources—on which modern technology is based—to be exhausted. Long-term interdependent strategies select for behaviors that are beneficial for the success of the whole group. As soon as the number of people participating in short-term strategies increases beyond a sustainable level, the population heads towards maladaptation.[149] Long-term interdependent strategies are **not** subject to frequency-dependency. They are enduring and self-sustaining strategies that continually re-adapt to changing circumstances. Abundance, diversity, and stability are continually re-created in a system of mutual interdependence between human society and the environment.

Each region can have its own autonomy, its own subsistence economy. Trade with different regions might be supplemental, but for the sake of sustainability, should **not** be **complemental**. Self-sufficiency within geographic regions was the manner in which the world's various cultures and their economic systems originated. Recreating this trend is the best chance we have to develop long-term successful strategies and to maintain the physical environment, the biologic environment, and our species as a whole, through the proper cultivation of our social environment.

---

148. Ibid., p. 378.
149. Barkow, Jerome, p. 377.

References

Altman, Irwin, <u>Culture and Environment</u>. Cambridge University Press, 1984.

Barkow, Jerome H., "The Elastic between Genes and Culture" in <u>Anthropological Theory</u>, R. Jon McGee and Richard Warms, eds., pps. 374-390. London: Mayfield Publishing Company, 1996.

Basch, Linda, Nina Glick Schiller, and Cristina Szanton Blanc, <u>Nations Unbound: Transnational Projects, Post-Colonial Predicaments, and Deterritorialized Nation-States</u>. Gordon & Breach Publishers, 1994.

Beach, Hugh, <u>Reindeer-Herd Management in Transition: The Case of Tuorpon Saameby in Northern Sweden</u>, LiberTryck, Stockholm, 1980.

Bock, Philip K., "Micmac." In *Handbook of North American Indians*, Vol. 15, *Northeast*, edited by Bruce G. Trigger, pp. 109-122. Washington D.C.: Smithsonian Institute, 1978.

Bornstein, Morris, Ed., <u>Comparative Economic Systems: Models and Cases</u>, 4th Edition. Richard D. Irwin, 1979.

Boyd, Robert and Peter J. Richerson, "Punishment Allows the Evolution of Cooperation (or Anything Else) in Sizable Groups", in *Ethology and Sociobiology*. Elsvier Science Publishing Company, 1992.

Campbell, Bernard, <u>Human Ecology</u>. Aldine Publishing Company, 1983.

Castetter, Edward F. and Willis H. Bell, <u>Yuman Indian Agriculture: Primitive Subsistence on the Lower Colorado and Gila Rivers</u>. University of New Mexico Press, 1951.

Chang, Kwang-Chih, <u>Fengpitou, Tapenkeng, and the Prehistory of Taiwan</u>. Department of Anthropology, Yale University, 1969.

Copper, John F., <u>Historical Dictionary of Taiwan</u>, from *Asian Historical Dictionaries*, No. 12, Edited by Jon Woronoff. The Scarecrow Press, Inc., 1993.

Damasio, Antonio, <u>DesCartes' Error: Emotion, Reason, and the Human Brain</u>. Copyright, Antonio R. Damasio, Inc., Avon Books, 1994.

Ekman, Paul, "Biological and Cultural Contributions to the Body and Facial Movement in the Expression of Emotions," in <u>Explaining Emotions</u>. Amelie Oksenberg Rorty Ed., University of California Press, 1980.

Fernea, Robert A. and Georg Gerster Ill., <u>Nubians in Egypt</u>. University of Texas Press, 1973.

Gellner, Ernest, <u>Nations And Nationalism</u>. Cornell University Press, 1983.

Giddens, Anthony, <u>The Consequences of Modernity</u>. Standford University Press, 1990.

Gonzalez, Ellice B., <u>Changing Economic Roles for Micmac Men and Women: An Ethnohistorical Analysis</u>. Canadian Ethnology Service, Paper no. 72. National Museum of Man, Ottawa, 1981.

Gregor, A. James, <u>Ideology and Development: Sun Yat-sen and the Economic History of Taiwan</u>. Institute of East Asian Studies, University of California, 1981.

Gudykunst, William B., <u>Bridging Differences: Effective Intergroup Communication</u>, 2nd Edition. SAGE Publications, 1994.

Halperin, Rhoda H., <u>Cultural Economies: Past and Present</u>. University of Texas Press, 1994.

Hannerz, Ulf, <u>Cultural Complexity: Studies in the Social Organization of Meaning</u>. Colombia University Press, 1992.

Hoffman, Bernard G., "The Historical Ethnography of the Micmac of the Sixteenth and Seventeenth Centuries." Ph.D. diss., University of California, Berkley, 1955.

Jagger, Alison M., "Love and Knowledge: Emotion in Feminist Epistemology," pp. 145-169, in Gender/Body/Knowledge. Alison M. Jagger and Susan Bordo Eds., Rutgers University Press, 1989.

Kroeber, A. L., Mohave Indians: Report on Aboriginal Territory and Occupancy of the Mohave Tribe. Garland Publishing Inc., 1974.

Leakey, Richard E., The Origin of Humankind. Copyright, Sherma, B. V., Published by BasicBooks, A Division of HarperCollins Publishers, Inc., 1994.

Leakey, Richard E., and Roger Lewin, People of the Lake: Mankind & Its Beginnings. Doubleday & Company, 1978.

LeBar, Frank M., Ed., "Part IV. Formosa." *Ethnic Groups of Insular Southeast Asia*, Vol. 2, *Philippines and Formosa*. Human Relations Area Files Press, 1975.

Li, Dr. Kwoh-ting, Economic Transformation of Taiwan. Shepheard-Walwyn Publishers Ltd., 1988.

McGaa, Ed "Eagle Man", Native Wisdom: Perceptions of the Natural Way. Four Directions Publishing, 1995.

Paine, Robert, Herds of the Tundra: A Portrait of Saami Reindeer Pastoralism. Smithsonian Institution Press, 1994.

Polanyi, Karl, Primitive, Archaic, and Modern Economies. Anchor Books, 1968.

Reader, John, Man on Earth. William Collins Sons & Co. Ltd., 1988 and University of Texas Press, 1988.

Ryle, Gilbert, "*From* The Concept of Mind," in What is an Emotion?, Cheshire Calhoun and Robert C. Solomon Eds., pp. 252-263. Oxford University Press, 1984.

Sahlins, Marshall, <u>Stone Age Economics</u>. Aldine Publishing Company, 1972.

Sherer, Lorraine M., <u>The Clan System of the Fort Mohave Indians</u>. The Historical Society of Southern California Indians, 1965.

Steward, Julian, <u>Theory of Culture Change</u>. University of Illinois Press, 1955.

Stewart, Kenneth M., "Mohave." In *Handbook of North American Indians*, Vol. 10, *Southwest*, edited by Alfonso Ortiz, pp. 55-70. Washington D.C.: Smithsonian Institute, 1983.

Tedlock, Dennis, <u>Popul Vuh: The Definitive Definition of the Mayan Book of the Dawn of Life and the Glories of Gods and Kings</u>, Revised Edition. Copyright, Dennis Tedlock, Simon & Schuster, 1996.

Upton, Leslie F. S., <u>Micmacs and Colonists: Indian-White Relations in the Maritimes</u>, 1713-1867. University of British Colombia Press, 1979.

Wallis, Wilson D. and Ruth S., <u>The Micmac Indians of Eastern Canada</u>. Minnesota Press, 1955.

Wolf, Margery, <u>The House of Lim: A Study of a Chinese Farm Family</u>. Appleton-Century-Crofts, A Division of Merredith Corporation, 1968.

Bibliography

Altman, Irwin, <u>Culture and Environment</u>. Cambridge University Press, 1984.

Barkow, Jerome H., "The Elastic between Genes and Culture" in <u>Anthropological Theory</u>, R. Jon McGee and Richard Warms, eds., pps. 374-390. London: Mayfield Publishing Company, 1996.

Basch, Linda, Nina Glick Schiller, and Cristina Szanton Blanc, <u>Nations Unbound: Transnational Projects, Post-Colonial Predicaments, and Deterritorialized Nation-States</u>. Gordon & Breach Publishers, 1994.

Beach, Hugh, <u>Reindeer-Herd Management in Transition: The Case of Tuorpon Saameby in Northern Sweden</u>, LiberTryck, Stockholm, 1980.

Black Hawk, in <u>Native American Wisdom</u>. Kent Nerburn and Louise Mengelkoch, Eds.. New World Library, 1991.

Bock, Philip K., "Micmac." In *Handbook of North American Indians,* Vol. 15, *Northeast*, edited by Bruce G. Trigger, pp. 109-122. Washington D.C.: Smithsonian Institute, 1978.

Bornstein, Morris, Ed., <u>Comparative Economic Systems: Models and Cases</u>, 4th Edition. Richard D. Irwin, 1979.

Boyd, Robert and Peter J. Richerson, "Punishment Allows the Evolution of Cooperation (or Anything Else) in Sizable Groups", in *Ethology and Sociobiology*. Elsvier Science Publishing Company, 1992.

Campbell, Bernard, <u>Human Ecology</u>. Aldine Publishing Company, 1983.

Castetter, Edward F. and Willis H. Bell, <u>Yuman Indian Agriculture: Primitive Subsistence on the Lower Colorado and Gila Rivers</u>. University of New Mexico Press, 1951.

Chang, Kwang-Chih, <u>Fengpitou, Tapenkeng, and the Prehistory of Taiwan</u>. Department of Anthropology, Yale University, 1969.

China Yearbook 1961-62, James C. H. SHEN, Chairman. Published by the China Publishing Company, Copyright 1962.

Copper, John F., <u>Historical Dictionary of Taiwan</u>, from *Asian Historical Dictionaries*, No. 12, Edited by Jon Woronoff. The Scarecrow Press, Inc., 1993.

Damasio, Antonio, <u>DesCartes' Error: Emotion, Reason, and the Human Brain</u>. Copyright, Antonio R. Damasio, Inc., Avon Books, 1994.

Eastman, Charles Alexander (Ohiyesa), in <u>Native American Wisdom</u>. Kent Nerburn and Louise Mengelkoch, Eds.. New World Library, 1991.

Ekman, Paul, "Biological and Cultural Contributions to the Body and Facial Movement in the Expression of Emotions," in <u>Explaining Emotions</u>. Amelie Oksenberg Rorty Ed., University of California Press, 1980.

Encyclopedia of Cultural Anthropology, David Levinson and Melvin Ember Eds.. Henry Holt & Co., 1996.

Encyclopedia of World Cultures, David Levinson Ed., G. K. Hall & Co., 1991.

Fernea, Robert A. and Georg Gerster Ill., <u>Nubians in Egypt</u>. University of Texas Press, 1973.

Gellner, Ernest, <u>Nations And Nationalism</u>. Cornell University Press, 1983.

Giddens, Anthony, <u>The Consequences of Modernity</u>. Standford University Press, 1990.

Gonzalez, Ellice B., <u>Changing Economic Roles for Micmac Men and Women: An Ethnohistorical Analysis</u>. Canadian Ethnology Service, Paper no. 72. National Museum of Man, Ottawa, 1981.

Gregor, A. James, <u>Ideology and Development: Sun Yat-sen and the Economic History of Taiwan</u>. Institute of East Asian Studies, University of California, 1981.

Gudykunst, William B., <u>Bridging Differences: Effective Intergroup Communication</u>, 2nd Edition. SAGE Publications, 1994.

Halperin, Rhoda H., <u>Cultural Economies: Past and Present</u>. University of Texas Press, 1994.

Hannerz, Ulf, <u>Cultural Complexity: Studies in the Social Organization of Meaning</u>. Colombia University Press, 1992.

Heilbroner, Robert L., <u>The Nature and Logic of Capitalism</u>. W. W. Norton & Company, 1985.

Hoffman, Bernard G., "The Historical Ethnography of the Micmac of the Sixteenth and Seventeenth Centuries." Ph.D. diss., University of California, Berkley, 1955.

Illustrated Encyclopedia of Mankind, The, Richard Carlisle Ed., Marshall Cavendish Co., 1990.

Jagger, Alison M., "Love and Knowledge: Emotion in Feminist Epistemology," pp. 145-169, in <u>Gender/Body/Knowledge</u>. Alison M. Jagger and Susan Bordo Eds., Rutgers University Press, 1989.

Kroeber, A. L., <u>Mohave Indians: Report on Aboriginal Territory and Occupancy of the Mohave Tribe</u>. Garland Publishing Inc., 1974.

Leakey, Richard E., <u>The Origin of Humankind</u>. Copyright, Sherma, B. V., Published by BasicBooks, A Division of HarperCollins Publishers, Inc., 1994.

Leakey, Richard E., and Roger Lewin, <u>People of the Lake: Mankind & Its Beginnings</u>. Doubleday & Company, 1978.

LeBar, Frank M., Ed., "Part IV. Formosa." *Ethnic Groups of Insular Southeast Asia*, Vol. 2, *Philippines and Formosa*. Human Relations Area Files Press, 1975.

Li, Dr. Kwoh-ting, <u>Economic Transformation of Taiwan</u>. Shepheard-Wal-wyn Publishers Ltd., 1988.

McGaa, Ed, <u>Native Wisdom: Perceptions of the Natural Way</u>. Four Directions Publishing, 1995.

New Encyclopaedia Britannica, The, 15th Edition, Jacob E. Safra, Chairman of the Board. Encyclopaedia Britannica, Inc., 1997.

Paine, Robert, <u>Herds of the Tundra: A Portrait of Saami Reindeer Pastoralism</u>. Smithsonian Institution Press, 1994.

Polanyi, Karl, <u>Primitive, Archaic, and Modern Economies</u>. Anchor Books, 1968.

Reader, John, <u>Man on Earth</u>. William Collins Sons & Co. Ltd., 1988 and University of Texas Press, 1988.

Republic of China Yearbook 1996, The, CHANG Ying Ed.. Government Information Office, 1996.

Ryle, Gilbert, "*From* <u>The Concept of Mind</u>," in <u>What is an Emotion?</u>, Cheshire Calhoun and Robert C. Solomon Eds., pp. 252-263. Oxford University Press, 1984.

Sahlins, Marshall, <u>Stone Age Economics</u>. Aldine Publishing Company, 1972.

Sherer, Lorraine M., <u>The Clan System of the Fort Mohave Indians</u>. The Historical Society of Southern California Indians, 1965.

Steward, Julian, <u>Theory of Culture Change</u>. University of Illinois Press, 1955.

Stewart, Kenneth M., "Mohave." In *Handbook of North American Indians*, Vol. 10, *Southwest*, edited by Alfonso Ortiz, pp. 55-70. Washington D.C.: Smithsonian Institute, 1983.

Tedlock, Dennis, <u>Popul Vuh: The Definitive Definition of the Mayan Book of the Dawn of Life and the Glories of Gods and Kings</u>, Revised Edition. Copyright, Dennis Tedlock, Simon & Schuster, 1996.

Thurman, Harold V., Essentials of Oceanography, 4th Edition. Macmillan Publishing Company, 1993.

Upton, Leslie F. S., Micmacs and Colonists: Indian-White Relations in the Maritimes, 1713-1867. University of British Colombia Press, 1979.

Wallis, Wilson D. and Ruth S., The Micmac Indians of Eastern Canada. Minnesota Press, 1955.

Wallace, Robert A., Gerald P. Sanders, and Robert J. Ferl, Biology: The Science of Life, 3rd Edition. Harper Collins Publishers, 1991.

Wolf, Margery, The House of Lim: A Study of a Chinese Farm Family. Appleton-Century-Crofts, A Division of Merredith Corporation, 1968.

World Book Encyclopedia, The, W. Richard Dell Ed.. World Book Inc., 1997.

Index

a part of 1, 8, 17 & 18.

abundance xiii, xiii(in numbers), xiv, 15, 21(in numbers), 22, 39, 43, & 54.

achieved xiv, 15, 27, 36, & 47.

advent 1.

agriculture(al) 1, 4 & 5, 7 & 8, 17(limited), 17(extensive), 17(intensive), 19(limited), 19, 19(extensive), 19(intensive), 19(economies), 22, 26(traditional), 27, 29(simple), 30-32, 32(economy), 32(limited), 33, 33(societies), 33(product), 34(modernized), 34(labor-intensive), 33(modernization, 35, 35(exports), 36, 40-42(ist(s)), 42(produce), 43(economy), 43, 43 & 44(production), 44(economy), 44(use), 47, 47(economies), & 49(ists).

alleviating 2.

alter xiv(ed), 1, 2(ing), 8, 8(ing), 15(ed), 20-21(ed), 20-21(ing), 21, 40, 44(ed), & 54(native).

alteration(s) xiii & xiv, 4, 15, 21, 34(massive), & 36.

ancestors 1.

apart from 1, 8, 17-19, & 45.

appropriate 13(ly), 48(socially), & 51.

archaic 1.

asocial 37.

aspect(s) xiii(social, physical, & biological), 4(various), 23(every), 28(all), 50(biological & physical), & 52(biological, physical & sociological).

Australopithecus 1(boisei).

autonomy 2, 9, & 54.

behavior(s) 3 & 4, 7 & 8, 8(al), 12, 12(mis), 12 & 13(immoral), 13 & 14(moral), 18 & 19, 24,

40(animals), 40(agriculturist group), 43(Asian peoples), 44(developing industrial nations), 47(confer with), 47(economic systems), 47, 48(take care of), 48(concerned for), 48(exploit the efforts of), 48(independent systems), 48(members of the group), 48(social relations of mutual love and respect for), 52(necessities of life), & 53(cultures).

other(s), each 10(between), 12(the environment and), 24('), 25(respect for), 28(relied on), 28(not to offend), 36(between), 36(depend on), 39(not really know), 39(biologically depend on), 43('), 47(treat), 48(pitted against), 48(dependent on), 48(depend on), & 53(dominate technologically).

other species(') xiii(relative abundance of), xiv(exploitation, endangerment and extinction of), xiv(high in domestication of), xiv(little exploitation and endangerment of), xiv(low in domestication of), 1(in relative harmony with), 1(in the environment), 1(on earth), 8(as below themselves), 9, 10(ultimately rely upon), 10(bonds between humans and), 10(needed connection between themselves and), 11(the mem-

bers of), 11 & 12, 14(dominating), 14, 14(extend outwards towards), 14(social bonds between humans and), 14(even biological bonds between), 17(harm to), 29(strong emotional bonds towards), 29(the Micmac and), 33(see themselves above), 36(among), 43(strong bonds between themselves and), 44(economies of), 45(economies), 48(members of the group and), 48(form), 49(emotionally sympathetic bond between members of the human species and), 49, 51(the "economic systems" of the), 53(develop the ability to dominate), 53(the needs of), & 53(allows).

owners 35(private).

ownership xiii & xiv(public), xiii(private), 15(private), & 20(private).

passively 8.

pastoral 26(production).

pastoral, procuring 21.

pastoral economies 18(full), & 18(two).

pastoral economy 25(interdependent) & 38.

pastoral societies, procuring 21.

About the Author

Recently graduated from the State University of New York at Buffalo with a Master's of Science in the Social Sciences Interdisciplinary Department. My concentration was in environment and cultural anthropology.

With the option of continuing on for my master's in the social sciences or study in some other related field, it seemed logical to remain in the social sciences. I utilized several branches of the social sciences, which aided me in pooling resources from a variety of angles to study the side-effects of various economic systems. This allowed me to realize where different disciplines could come together to analyze phenomenon from different perspectives, giving me the rare ability to formulate original theories on old problems.

Hopefully my perspective will be helpful to understanding the myriad of dilemmas the world faces today.